"The enemy seeks to rob us of our poten[...] by uprooting us from where God has p[...] designed to prepare us for what God has planned for us. In *Hope after Church Hurt*, Joe Dobbins helps readers find purpose through their pain so they can avoid the trap of offense, find healing, and fulfill their God-given destiny."

John Bevere, bestselling author and minister;
cofounder, Messenger International and MessengerX

"*Hope after Church Hurt* will speak life, hope, and healing to those who have been hurt by someone in the church. This resource will help you recover from the pain and lead you toward your purpose."

Jentezen Franklin, senior pastor, Free Chapel;
New York Times bestselling author

"Joe Dobbins, a friend and an amazing pastor, offers a diagnosis, prescription, and reentry plan to help you or someone you love heal from church hurt. As each of us gets healthier, we help the church get healthier and in turn help the world. This is a book I recommend every pastor have available to give to the wounded."

Tommy Barnett, pastor, Dream City Church, Phoenix;
pastor, Los Angeles Dream Center

"Zechariah's prophecy mentions 'the wounds I was given at the house of my friends' (Zechariah 13:6). Although we believe this prophecy speaks of Jesus' experience on the cross, it also speaks of our experience in life. Many times life wounds are inflicted by our 'spiritual friends' in church. How do we handle these hurts? How can we be healed? Pastor Joe addresses both our wounds and healing in *Hope after Church Hurt*."

Dr. Billy Wilson, president, Oral Roberts University;
chair, Empowered21 and Pentecostal World Fellowship

"Unfortunately, church hurt is real and something that anyone involved in ministry for any length of time has witnessed. Joe Dobbins calls upon his life experience to address this critical topic and offers multiple pathways to ease the repercussions associated with it."

Bishop Tim Hill, general overseer, Church of God, Cleveland, Tennessee

"I love Jesus and still believe in the church. I am excited about Joe's new book because I know it will bring hope and healing to every believer. God has an awesome plan for our lives, and He will greatly use the church to accomplish that plan. I know the Lord will use this book to help us step into an amazing future!"

Jabin Chavez, senior pastor, City Light Church, Las Vegas

"One of the most pervasive hidden pains in our world today is the pain of past church hurt. When we feel abandoned, judged, used, or abused by people we trusted within the church, the scars can be long-lasting and the road to recovery can feel uncertain. My friend Pastor Joe Dobbins understands church hurt, and his book is a safe refuge for anyone who is dealing with these scars. Joe is one of the most authentic and inspiring Jesus followers I've ever known. He's the real deal. This book beautifully blends biblical truth, real-life stories, and creative strategies to illuminate a pathway toward healing. If you've been hurt in the church, know that you matter. Your story matters. God has not forgotten about you. He still has a beautiful plan for you. I wholeheartedly believe this book could be a turning point in your journey toward healing."

Dave Willis, pastor and author

HOPE
after
Church Hurt

HOPE
after
Church Hurt

How to Heal, Reengage, and
Rediscover God's Heart for You

JOE DOBBINS

Chosen
a division of Baker Publishing Group
Minneapolis, Minnesota

Published by Chosen Books
Minneapolis, Minnesota
ChosenBooks.com

Chosen Books is a division of
Baker Publishing Group, Grand Rapids, Michigan

Printed in the United States of America

Library of Congress Cataloging-in-Publication Data
Names: Dobbins, Joe, author.
Title: Hope after church hurt : how to heal, reengage, and rediscover God's heart for you / Joe Dobbins.
Description: Minneapolis, Minnesota : Chosen Books, a division of Baker Publishing Group, [2024] | Includes bibliographical references.
Identifiers: LCCN 2023051438 | ISBN 9780800772642 (paper) | ISBN 9780800772659 (casebound) | ISBN 9781493446773 (ebook)
Subjects: LCSH: Psychology, Religious | Spiritual life—Christianity. | Psychic trauma—Religious aspects. | Psychological abuse—Religious aspects. | Control (Psychology)
Classification: LCC BL53.5 .D63 2024 | DDC 248.8/6—dc23/eng/20231117
LC record available at https://lccn.loc.gov/2023051438

Pathway Press edition ISBN 9780800772970

Cover design by Darren Welch

Baker Publishing Group publications use paper produced from sustainable forestry practices and postconsumer waste whenever possible.

24 25 26 27 28 29 30   7 6 5 4 3 2 1

To Mom and Dad
Thank you for your unending support and for raising me in church.

Contents

Part Three: Reengaging with Fresh Faith

Foreword

In life, we often find ourselves in places we never imagined, facing challenges we never expected. But within those challenges lies the potential for profound growth and transformation. *Hope after Church Hurt* is a compass guiding us through the often tumultuous landscape of spiritual pain toward a horizon aglow with hope, healing, and restoration.

I've come to know Joe not just as a writer but as a beacon of resilience and faith. Joe doesn't shy away from the raw and real experiences that many have encountered within the context of their faith communities. He dives headfirst into the complexities of church hurt, offering not only empathy but practical wisdom forged in the fires of his own struggles.

Wounds inflicted within the walls of our churches from broken trust, dashed hopes, or misguided actions can leave a soul adrift, questioning faith and wrestling with disillusionment. Yet Joe issues a clarion call, a beckoning toward a brighter tomorrow. He reminds us that in the midst of the hurt, there exists a path forward, one illuminated by the very love and compassion that drew us to faith in the first place.

Hope after Church Hurt isn't just a road map to recovery; it's an invitation to rediscover the essence of faith and the love of Christ—a love that transcends the failures of flawed institutions and imperfect people. It's a reminder that the core of our faith lies in the unyielding grace of God, a grace that not only forgives but empowers us to heal and extend grace to others.

Joe's insights serve as a guiding light, gently leading us from the shadows of pain into the radiance of restoration. He doesn't offer easy solutions or trite platitudes. Instead, he shares profound truths and practical steps to navigate the journey toward healing. His words resonate with empathy, understanding, and an unwavering belief in the redemptive power of faith.

This book is a reminder that our scars don't define us, but rather serve as testaments to our strength in Jesus Christ and His power to transform our pain and past hurt. May this book be a source of solace for the hurting, a catalyst for healing, and a clarion call for all of us to embrace hope amid our deepest wounds.

My prayer is that you find solace, restoration, and a renewed sense of purpose within these pages and that it draws you back into the body of Christ. Let the journey toward hope and healing begin.

Pastor Samuel Rodriguez, New Season Church of Sacramento;
author, *Persevere with Power* and *Your Mess, God's Miracle*

Introduction

More than ever, I appreciate sitting with someone over coffee and hearing their story. Some time ago, I sat down with an Americano and a friend I'll call Sam. If you met Sam, you'd love him. He's kind, intelligent, and a great conversationalist. The agenda for our time together was simple—I wanted to hear more about his faith.

After a few minutes of small talk, I said, "Tell me about your experience with church." Sam's body language suddenly changed. He sat up straight, took a deep breath, and started telling me how he grew up in a vibrant church community where people passionately worshiped God. He talked about the pastor's ability to make the Bible relevant and how much the student ministry had positively impacted him during his teenage years.

After Sam graduated high school, his most significant relationships still revolved around this community, and he devoted a great deal of time to serving as a volunteer. Every word communicated how much Sam loved this church.

But all that changed the day his dad abruptly packed up Sam's younger siblings and his mother and announced they were moving, both from the area and away from the church. Sam didn't understand. For as long as he could remember, his family had been the model of perfection—like the one you'd see on the front of a church directory. But their departure was cloaked in mystery and confusion.

A few weeks later all uncertainty was cleared away when a series of selfish and damaging decisions his father had made came to light. And as more information rose to the surface and pressures increased, Sam's father grew defensive, eventually abandoning his family.

That was just the beginning of Sam's head-spinning season. Within six months, he'd lost not only his intact family and childhood home but his job. This ushered in a season of severe depression and thoughts of self-harm, causing him to drift away from his friends and church. But Sam's absence seemed to go unnoticed, as no one from the church reached out for months.

Finally, a staff pastor suggested they meet for lunch. Sam told me, "The relief I felt was palpable. I was barely holding it together, and then someone reached out and showed they cared." Sam felt hope for the first time in a long while.

He arrived at the restaurant early, not wanting to miss a moment of what he was sure would be a life-giving conversation. More than anything, he wanted to hear someone say everything would be OK, that God still had a plan. And that even though his earthly dad had failed him, his heavenly Father still loved him and never would.

Sadly, those were not the words Sam heard. Before he could share everything happening to his family or what was going on in his heart, the pastor expressed how disappointed he was with him. He was frustrated that Sam had pulled back from serving, hadn't displayed more faith, didn't have a job, and had no plan for his life.

As you might imagine, Sam was shocked. He told me, "I did my best to blink away tears. I just couldn't believe what I was hearing. After being berated by this pastor for things over which I had no control, I didn't know if I'd have the strength to make it through another day."

Lunch ended along with the pastor's lecture. And as Sam left the restaurant, he also left the idea of church. He resigned from all his positions, and for the next decade he avoided anything that looked like church. In his mind, life was hard enough without being hurt from the place that was supposed to help him.

Stories like Sam's are why this book exists. I'm not naïve to think church could ever be a utopia where pain or conflict cease. The fact is as long as churches are made up of people, they'll never be perfect. But I am concerned that the place that should be known for lifting burdens is too often known for adding to them.

Is that your experience? Have you experienced pain in the one place you least expected it? If your answer is yes, then know I wrote this book for you.

Before we begin this journey toward inner healing, let me share a few things from my heart. I hope they'll provide a filter for what you read and help you get the most out of what's ahead.

First, please know I'm sorry for what happened to you. Although the details of your story are unique, in the same way my heart broke for Sam, it breaks for you.

Second, I've done my best to compassionately bring you hope on a broad level, but there was simply no way I could include every negative experience when it comes to church hurt. So if yours isn't covered here—or some of its nuances are missing—don't be discouraged. The Holy Spirit can take this message and apply it to your heart in a customized way.

Third, I apologize for the hurt I've caused. At times I've been selfish, inconsiderate, gossipy, judgmental, and more. I've caused others pain, and I think writing this book without admitting that fact would be disingenuous and defeat the purpose.

Finally, in order to truly gain all this book has to offer, you must be honest with yourself about what happened to you and the current condition of your soul. In Psalm 119:29, the psalmist says to the Lord, "Keep me from lying to myself" (NLT). That's a necessary prayer, because we're all capable of ignoring what's hurting us or making excuses for failing to make changes for the better.

I know an entire book about your most painful experiences—even though healing is the goal—can seem overwhelming. That's one reason I've broken this one into three parts:

First, I outline why it's important to assess the damage you endured, especially if you've been ignoring or burying it rather than dealing with it. Second, I explain how you can find God's path to healing whatever your hurt, with step-by-step encouragement. And third, I share how you can best reengage with a fresh faith, safely serving alongside God's people as He intends. And after each chapter, I offer a personal prayer to give you the words to signal to God you're inviting His work and want to move forward.

Now, if you believe you've already identified your hurt as one of the ones I cover in this book, you may be tempted to skip ahead to a chapter dedicated to it. But consider resisting that temptation for two reasons:

Your hurt could be multifaceted. It might surprise you to discover you don't have a single hurt with a single source. For example, you could be hurt by both judgmentalism *and* rejection. Or by unresolved conflict *and* wounding words. Inner wounds often have a compounding effect, and there is no doubt God wants to heal every layer of the hurt you've experienced.

It's for that reason I am encouraging you to go through this book from the beginning. Part One sets a foundation for why taking this journey is so important—perhaps in ways that haven't occurred to you. I believe if you start at the beginning with an open heart, you will arrive at the end with a healed heart.

Understanding a little about others' wounds might help you aid in their healing journey. Chances are you know someone else who's experienced church hurt, and I believe you can play a critical part in helping them heal. You'll need to wait for an invitation or God's leading, but readiness is key to standing by others who need support.

I'm grateful to say that all these years later, Sam has been honest with himself about his wound and took the steps needed to recover. Today, he's passionately in love with Jesus, holds no resentment, and is reengaged in a faith community where he helps others find hope each week. His story reinforces the reality that there's real healing in Christ and the church still has purpose.

Despite what one or more of His followers may have done to you, Jesus remains your biggest fan, best friend, and the only path to true peace. He's not giving up on you or His church—and there's hope! Both can be healed and used to heal others.

PART ONE

✝

Assessing the Damage You've Endured

1

It's Time to Tackle the Problem

"I love Jesus, but I can't stand His people!"

That statement hit me like a ton of bricks as I listened to a woman in her mid-fifties. She described how years ago she'd endured painful comments about the way she dressed, how she parented, and the state of her marriage from women deemed "spiritually mature." Their words were so wounding that she'd begun second-guessing her faith and had stopped attending church altogether. In fact, she was standing in the lobby of our church talking to me only because the pressures of her divorce finalizing and her daughter's declining behavior had brought her to a place of desperation.

As I listened to her, my heart ached not only for her present predicament but for her past pain. She'd been wounded where she was supposed to be healed. She'd been criticized by people who were supposed to encourage her. And she'd lost her faith in the very institution that exists to help people find it.

Like millions of others, her story is wrapped up in a phrase that's become all too common and all too familiar—*church hurt*. So universal is this phrase that it's trended on social media, headlined countless news stories, and been the subject of documentaries. And yet as popular as this phrase may be, it seems so strange. These two words should be diametrically opposed, yet they accurately describe the experience of so many.

Church Hurt Is Age-Old and Widespread

From the time of the Bible's book of Acts to the Middle Ages, the Reformation, and each great awakening, we have examples of God's people acting in ungodly ways. Even some of our most esteemed leaders have fallen victim to what we now call church hurt.

John Wesley led great revivals in the 1700s, and he was so influential that many of the institutions and practices he founded are still shaping the landscape of faith today. And his ability to preach was so piercing that he drew crowds of astonishing size. Yet as stunning as his success was, so was his opposition. In one diary entry he wrote that within a two-month period he was rejected by seven different churches. After speaking in one of them, the deacons asked that he never return, and in another church, the board told him, "Get out and stay out." Even worse, in an outdoor church meeting, someone released a bull to attack him!

So although some might think church hurt is a new problem, let me assure you that the church has been dysfunctional for centuries.

No matter the label, theology, or denomination, not one faith community has been unaffected by this issue. People of all ages and walks of life as well as of every level of commitment have endured pain in a place of worship. If you want proof, look no further than recent headlines. The oldest church in the world remains entrenched in scandals, while simultaneously some of the world's most modern churches are struggling to navigate their own issues.

Indeed, church hurt is a dysfunction that knows no boundaries and chooses no favorites.

I'm No Stranger to Church Hurt

My wife, Kayla, and I both grew up in the church, and some of our best memories come from being with God's people. At the same time, we've had to deal with our own wounds from followers of Christ.

One of the most impactful events came during our engagement. We were in our early twenties, and Kayla's parents had some concerns about our age and how fast our relationship had progressed. Their initial response to our plan to marry was not what we'd hoped—they opposed the idea, which launched us all into a difficult season.

Kayla was particularly torn because she wanted to both honor her parents and marry me, and in this tension she sincerely wanted God's guidance. So she decided to press into her faith. One Sunday during a service at her church, she found a place to kneel and pray as people worshiped God.

Typically when a person took such a step, someone within the church came alongside and prayed with them. So it wasn't surprising when an active and influential church member approached. Of course, Kayla assumed this was an act of compassion or an attempt to comfort her, but it was quite the opposite. Apparently, this member had heard about her family's turmoil and decided they'd fix it by lecturing Kayla in front of the whole church, accusing her of acting in rebellion toward her parents through pursuing an ungodly relationship with me.

Obviously, Kayla was confused because this was someone who was supposed to represent God's loving guidance. She was also crushed because she felt as though she had lost the one place that was supposed to be safe to struggle. That experience wounded us both, and we carried the effects of anger, rejection, and distrust for years.

What's *Your* Story?

Though I've not had the privilege of hearing your story, I'm reasonably sure you have one. That's because if you've followed Jesus for any amount of time, it's likely you've been hurt by at least one of His followers. Maybe you've:

- endured the exclusion cliques create.
- been pierced by judgmental remarks.
- learned someone you admired was a fraud.
- been a victim of gossip.
- been made to feel less than because of your past.
- been used for your gifts but not loved as a person.
- been misled by leaders or abandoned by people you thought were friends.
- been abused by someone in authority and made to feel it was your fault.

The details of each person's story are different, but the pain is the same. If you've been wounded in a place of worship, Kayla and I understand. And from that understanding, I feel an urgency to help. For too long, offenses, abuses, and unresolved issues within faith communities have been minimized, sanitized, and swept under the rug. These actions have resulted in churches lacking power because they're reeling from untreated pain.

It's time to take an honest look within. It's time to have an open conversation about what happened. It's time to tackle the problem.

Broadening Our Understanding of the Body of Christ

For years, people in faith communities have been categorized in one of two ways: believer or unbeliever, Christian or non-Christian, lost or found, saved or unsaved. The longer I lead a faith community, however, the more I realize there's an ever-growing third category of people who, like the woman I listened to in the lobby that day, love Jesus yet struggle with the church.

One research project in the last decade revealed that nearly sixty-five million Americans were once involved in church but then left.[1] That's approximately the same number who still regularly attended. Clearly, the faith community can no longer be classified into two columns but three: non-Christian, connected Christian, and disconnected Christian.

One day this reality jumped off the page as I read one of the most familiar stories in Scripture, commonly referred to as the parable of the lost sheep. Jesus said:

> If a man owns a hundred sheep, and one of them wanders away, will he not leave the ninety-nine on the hills and go to look for the one that wandered off? And if he finds it, truly I tell you, he is happier about that one sheep than about the ninety-nine that did not wander off. In the same way your Father in heaven is not willing that any of these little ones should perish.
>
> Matthew 18:12–14

Sometimes a passage like this is presented in such a way that we miss the context. For example, when this parable is retold, it's often with the idea that the ninety-nine sheep are believers and the one sheep is the rogue sinner who needs to get right with God. But that interpretation ignores the fact that Jesus never mixed analogies, because He wanted to avoid any confusion among His followers. Imagine how hard it would be to interpret His teachings if in one parable something was good and in another parable it was bad.

Now, with that in mind, consider that whenever Jesus used sheep in an analogy, they represented those in relationship with Him. In contrast, goats always represented those not in relationship with Him. So if this parable in Matthew 18 were about ninety-nine believers and one sinner, the believers would be represented by one type of animal and the sinner by another. The story would be about the ninety-nine sheep and the heathen goat.

But all one hundred animals are sheep, and they all belong to the shepherd. So this parable isn't about saved and unsaved people; it's about ninety-nine connected people who love the Shepherd and one disconnected person who loves the Shepherd but struggles to stay in the fold.

Now that we have a clearer understanding of this Scripture, let's answer two vital questions.

Why did this one sheep disconnect from the others?

Could it have been offended because a certain sheep was sweet on stage but acted like a goat backstage? Maybe someone said this sheep should get control of her lambs while the shepherd was speaking. Perhaps another sheep's insensitive political post made this sheep wander away. Or maybe this sheep was criticized for not wearing a modest cut of wool.

The truth is we don't know why this sheep wandered. But we do know at some point it started following its feelings instead of the shepherd's voice, and the result was separation and isolation.

What would motivate the shepherd to leave ninety-nine to find one?

Last time I checked, a positive 99 percent was pretty good. If you had a hundred dollars and lost a single one-dollar bill, I doubt you would lose sleep or reprioritize your entire day just to find it. So why is this shepherd so concerned about one animal that he's halted progress and started searching? I believe it's because he knows the danger that accompanies being disconnected.

When we experience physical pain, it's natural to simply react. If you touch a hot stove, you don't take an intellectual approach and consider the scientific realities of what's happening. You just pull your hand away.

Our hearts are no different when they experience pain. When we hear a hurtful comment or learn we've been misled, we simply react by pulling away. The problem is we fail to realize that dangers come from our decision to disengage from a community of faith.

Four Dangers of Disconnecting

Let's examine four ways we become vulnerable when we disconnect.

1. We're uncovered.

Just because you're part of the flock doesn't mean life is without storms. But it is easier and safer to endure the elements when you're not alone. Like countless others, you may be going through a storm in your marriage, finances, or family, and it's brutal because you're enduring it on your own. You're not covered in prayer, not covered with encouragement, and not covered by wise voices to help you navigate this season. You're experiencing greater difficulty because you're uncovered.

2. We're unprotected.

I don't know whether you've ever watched the National Geographic network, but in our house, we've seen nearly every documentary. I've learned the migration patterns of blue whales, the building skills of beavers, and how hippos get a mate. That said, something even a novice Nat Geo viewer understands is if you leave the flock, you're a target for predators. It's never the sheep in the center of the flock that gets eaten; it's the one that's been separated.

I don't know where your faith is, but please lean into this reality: whether or not you believe it, you have a spiritual enemy. That's why God tells us through His Word, "Stay alert! Watch out for your great enemy, the devil. He prowls around like a roaring lion, looking for someone to devour" (1 Peter 5:8 NLT).

Notice Peter did not say "*God's* enemy." He said, "*Your* enemy." Now, you're probably thinking, *Joe, I'm not important enough to be on the devil's radar.* Please realize you don't have to be important for Satan to hate you. Because you carry God's image, he's hated you ever since your first breath. He's committed his entire existence to stealing, killing, and destroying your life. He's never had a moment of compassion toward you. In short, one of the reasons life may be so difficult is that you're under spiritual attack.

I wish I could tell you this will end, but it won't. Your enemy is unrelenting, and if you're disconnected, you're unprotected.

3. We're unkept.

Some years ago, the world was introduced to Shrek the sheep. At some point, Shrek wandered off from his fold and spent six years living alone in caves. You may have seen his photo on the news, because when they found him, he was overgrown to the point that he could barely move. When nearly sixty pounds of wool was sheared from his body, Shrek got a new lease on life. All those years of being unkept had caused him to carry an enormous weight.[2]

Similarly, some of us carry enormous weight in our souls. For some it's shame, for others stress, and still for others the consequences of sin. Whatever the case, it's weighing us down, but we can't shed it on our own because God created us to need others' help.

The truth is I have blind spots I can see only through the eyes of others. To remain spiritually healthy, I need other people to help me see some parts of my soul. I need leaders who can use God's Word like a scalpel to cut away wrong thinking. I need friends the Spirit can use to wash away my fear with encouragement. I need compassionate people who can clear away the guilt blocking my vision. But if I live at a distance from others, I stay weighed down.

4. We're unsure of God's love.

One of the best things about the season of life I'm in is that I live in a house full of kids. There's never a dull moment because they're always playing a game or using their imaginations. One of their favorite games is the classic hide-and-seek. You remember the premise: everyone hides within a designated area, and then one person (the one who's "it") searches for them. The game is simple and fun, but occasionally one of the hiders hides so well that the others give up trying to find them. The players already found move on to other activities, and the one forgotten emerges with hurt feelings.

I think that's how many people feel after experiencing church hurt. When they were initially wounded, they pulled back and hid. Then as time passed, the original wound was compounded by the pain of feeling forgotten. In some cases, the person has held the hurt so long that they feel as though even God has stopped looking for them, content with the ninety-nine who stayed.

If you feel that way, you couldn't be further from the truth. As a matter of fact, I believe the central message of the parable of the lost sheep is to communicate that church hurt holds a special place in God's heart. We think of shepherding almost like modern-day ranching, where cattle are processed like nameless numbers. But in Bible times, shepherds and sheep shared an intimate bond. A shepherd would nurse the sheep in their youth, carry them in sickness, watch over them as they slept, and sacrifice himself to protect them from harm. To the shepherd, not one sheep was expendable.

You can run, you can hide, but you can't get God to stop searching for your heart.

God's involvement with humanity is a story of hide-and-seek, only we get confused about who's "it." It was God the Father who went looking for Adam and Eve in the garden of Eden after they sinned (Genesis 3:9). Likewise, it was Jesus who went looking for the disciples after they'd abandoned Him in the garden of Gethsemane (John 20:19). Today, it's the Holy Spirit who's been looking for you (John 6:44). You can run, you can hide, but you can't get God to stop searching for your heart. He loves you too much to let you settle for less than His best.

He won't let you settle in isolation. Why? Because He has a family for you.

He won't let you settle in pain. Why? Because He has a purpose for you.

And He won't let you settle in the past. Why? Because He secured your future on the cross.

It's time to come out of hiding. It's time to tackle the problem. It's time to give in to the reality that God loves you unconditionally, obsessively, and eternally!

Healing Begins with Jesus' Leading

I'm sure just taking the time to start reading this chapter was a huge step if the pain you endured was and still is overwhelming. In fact, these few pages on a topic so personal may seem too simplistic to help bring about healing from the wound you've carried for perhaps decades.

Nevertheless, I want you to know that no relationship—even the one between you and His church—is so broken that God cannot heal it. When we genuinely open our hearts and allow God's Word and Spirit to access our pain, something supernatural happens. And I believe you're reading this because you're ready for supernatural healing.

As we move forward, this journey will take you through many topics and bring up memories of past hurts. But the first step to healing is deciding to let God—not your pain—call the shots and lead the way.

Jesus Will Always Lead You to Reengage the Church

For those who've endured church hurt, a common sentiment is, "I want Jesus, but I can do without the church." I've heard it a thousand times. The phrasing varies, but in essence people claim to be following Jesus but forgo connection to the church. On the surface that seems reasonable, but a harder look reveals a problem with this perspective.

Today, there's a great deal of debate about the relevancy of the church. Is it or is it not essential? Furthermore, in the wake of multiple moral failures and crippling corruption, many have given up on the church.

But Jesus isn't one of them! Ephesians 5:25 says, "Christ loved the church and gave himself up for her." In other words, Jesus died for the church, so why would He lead people away from the institution for which He paid the ultimate price? The Bible also tells us, "Christ is the head of the church, his body, of which he is the Savior" (Ephesians 5:23). This passage clearly lets us know Jesus hasn't resigned from His work with the church or passed the baton of leadership to someone else. He's still using what He's leading.

Additionally, the Scriptures repeatedly inform us that Christ is working through the church. For instance, God heals through gifts He's placed in the church (1 Corinthians 12:7–11), He guides through leaders He's placed in the church (Ephesians 4:12), He cares through the members of the church (Galatians 6:2), and He unlocks destiny through serving in the church (Romans 12:4–6).

These examples make it clear that asking God to move in your life without the church is like asking a carpenter to build without a hammer or a surgeon to heal without a scalpel.

Jesus Will Always Lead You to Release your Pain

This may be hard to hear, but I have to ask because it's part of being honest with yourself. Have you become proficient at reasoning away the need to release your pain? Have you learned to hide it, spiritualize it, ignore it, or even excuse it? We often do this not only to ease our pain but to justify the grudge we hold. In our resentment, we can even decide we'll love Jesus but stay away from His people.

If you've done any of this, you probably don't realize its high price. The Bible says, "Whoever claims to love God yet hates a brother or sister is a liar" (1 John 4:20). Did you catch that? Holding a grudge keeps our relationship with God from growing. I'm not saying your hurt was trivial, nor am I saying it didn't happen. I'm saying you must let go of the grudge in order to grow spiritually.

This is true for every believer who's been hurt, including those who haven't dismissed attending church but instead have disengaged their heart from being an active part of it. Maybe that's you.

You attend, but your heart isn't open to receive or contribute. Yet church isn't meant to be a spectator sport. You can go every Sunday but remain spiritually weak. At some point, you have to release your pain and reengage with God's people so He can begin working in your life again.

Don't Give Up

God's people may have hurt you, but God's heart is to heal you.

The months that followed Kayla's painful encounter at her church were trying, to say the least. We had to navigate confusion, rejection, anger, and a deep sense of grief. But today our hearts are at peace, and we hold nothing against the person who hurt us.

If you asked me how we found our way back to faith and the church, I'd tell you we just kept showing up. Often, we mistakenly believe it's our responsibility to restore ourselves, that the burden of healing falls squarely on our own shoulders. But healing is Jesus' responsibility, and not quitting is ours. When we simply keep showing up—little by little, week after week, prayer after prayer—we give God all He needs to transform our lives. So as you begin down this path and tackle your own problem, frequently return to the fact that there's great power in not giving up.

Heavenly Father, I'm finally ready to be honest, to heal, and to follow You. I ask for the tenacity necessary to work through the message of this book and to move into the life You created for me to live. In Jesus' name, amen.

2

Sometimes Life Just
Falls to Pieces

Putting puzzles together isn't my favorite activity, but from time to time my wife convinces me to join her in doing just that. One of the most memorable was a 750-piece Disney puzzle that depicted the hall of princesses. It didn't take long for my patience to wear thin as the task became pure princess torture! But after I bailed, Kayla kept connecting each tiny piece, and by evening she had only a handful left to complete the puzzle.

The next morning, I woke up before Kayla did, and as I descended the stairs, I could tell our preschool-aged daughter had already come down. When I rounded the corner and glanced at the table where the puzzle was, I couldn't believe my eyes. There she was grinning from ear to ear with pieces scattered everywhere. A "toddler tornado" had struck, and I felt like the first person to arrive at the scene of the disaster. All those hours were gone, and all the effort was lost. Only piles of pieces were left.

Isn't that just like life? No matter who you are or what you've accomplished, a moment comes when your life unexpectedly falls to pieces. For some, it comes in the form of losing a cherished position or experiencing a devastating financial setback. For others, it comes in the form of a sudden death or a breakup you never thought would happen. It can come in the form of abuse, addiction, or a negative diagnosis.

And for many, the trauma can be traced to a place they never would have expected—a church. After all, churches are the last place we expect our life to be shattered; that's where we go to be strengthened. Yet person after person can testify that their heart was broken when they were with people of faith.

If that's your experience, it breaks my heart to think you found pain instead of peace—and it breaks God's heart too. I believe that's why He's orchestrated your life to intersect with this message. At this point in your journey, you may feel like a part of you has died. If so, remember you serve a God who specializes in resurrections! He's an expert at rebuilding and restoring, and He'll bring you through this difficult season.

The Day David's Life Was Shattered

David was the second king of Israel, and though he's most well-known for his victories, he also had his share of defeats. In 2 Samuel 12, we get a detailed look at one of the lowest points in David's life. The tragedy began when he shrugged off his responsibility as king, and instead of leading his men on the battlefield, he chose to remain in the palace.

David was in the wrong place at the wrong time, and it led to one of the biggest mistakes of his life—an affair that resulted in pregnancy. David tried to hide his sin through a series of deceptions that ended with his ensuring that the woman's innocent husband was killed in battle and then taking her as a wife. But the Lord knew all this and was displeased, and David's guilt mounted. Add to all this, the new baby was born with a serious illness.

It seemed as though things couldn't get worse, but they did:

David pleaded with God for the child. He fasted and spent the nights lying in sackcloth on the ground. The elders of his household stood beside him to get him up from the ground, but he refused, and he would not eat any food with them. On the seventh day the child died. David's attendants were afraid to tell him that the child was dead, for they thought, "While the child was still living, he wouldn't listen to us when we spoke to him. How can we now tell him the child is dead? He may do something desperate."

2 Samuel 12:16–18

The English language fails to adequately express what David felt: heavy shame from sin, a strangling fear of losing the kingdom, and wave after wave of grief from the loss. David's world had fallen to pieces, and his servants were wondering how he would respond. But the Bible specifically tells us what he did:

Then David got up from the ground. After he had washed, put on lotions and changed his clothes, he went into the house of the LORD and worshiped. Then he went to his own house, and at his request they served him food, and he ate. His attendants asked him, "Why are you acting this way? While the child was alive, you fasted and wept, but now that the child is dead, you get up and eat!" He answered, "While the child was still alive, I fasted and wept. I thought, 'Who knows? The LORD may be gracious to me and let the child live.' But now that he is dead, why should I go on fasting? Can I bring him back again? I will go to him, but he will not return to me." Then David comforted his wife Bathsheba, and he went to her and made love to her. She gave birth to a son, and they named him Solomon. The LORD loved him.

2 Samuel 12:20–24

I think we can all agree that these events had the capacity to end David's sanity, yet he survived to see better days. I'll show you essential steps he took to get these results, but first notice what David didn't do. *He didn't insist on knowing why the tragedy happened.*

I bring this up because when we go through trauma, our typical response is to try to identify why it happened and who's to blame. But David didn't invest energy in seeking those answers.

This is a subtle but significant observation, because often our healing never starts because our questions never end. I understand the reason you ask *why*, but I've learned that when it comes to pain, explanations don't help. If I were to drop dead tomorrow and my wife knew the reason, it wouldn't lessen her grief. When our hearts are broken, we don't need answers; we need healing.

> *When our hearts are broken, we don't need answers; we need healing.*

David recovered because in the wake of his collapse he trusted that God is good despite the circumstances being bad. Your response to hard seasons determines a great deal about your future. If you decide to trust God, you'll grow in faith and deepen your relationship with Him. But if you close your heart, you'll drown in doubts, be buried in burdens, and feel far from the only One who can heal you. Our deepest hurts can be healed only by God, but God can heal only those who trust Him.

Four Steps to Trusting God in the Wake of Tragedy

So what does trust look like when your head is still spinning from your life falling to pieces? Like David, you can take four specific steps to settle the chaos and put your faith in a position for reconstruction.

1. Tell God how you really feel.

The Bible says when David's child was sick, he spent day and night in sackcloth, a cultural way of that day to openly mourn. He didn't put on a happy face or go around posting inspirational quotes; he mourned. He was gut-level honest with God and told Him, "I'm hurting, I'm depressed, I'm discouraged, and I'm having doubts."

As human beings, we have a problem being upfront and honest, and it isn't a new problem. This tendency has been passed down since the beginning. As soon as the original sin was committed, Adam and Eve hid in the garden. Then their son Cain denied knowing what happened to his brother, Abel, whom he'd killed in the field. Years later, Abraham claimed his wife was his sister to protect himself, Joseph's brothers covered up their selling him into slavery, and Moses buried the Egyptian he murdered.

What was true of those before us is true of us—honesty is a struggle.

One of the biggest mistakes I see people in pain make is thinking they have to keep up appearances with God. That to be "spiritual" means a commitment to grin and bear it for God's glory. But the truth is as long as we're "acting," God is not. We have to be real with Him in order to experience His restoration.

I want you to know God is big enough to hear how you feel, and His love isn't so flimsy that it will break under the weight of your anger or disappointment. At times, I think we forget that God created our emotions, including mourning. When we mourn, we express our hurt to Him and release the pain. If you don't release your pain, you'll carry it forever.

Mourning is also how you receive God's comfort. Jesus said, "Blessed are those who mourn, for they will be comforted" (Matthew 5:4). Until you mourn, you can't receive God's peace, strength, and comfort. This is why so many people never sit quietly with the Lord. When we do, He often brings up the pain we've tried to hide or ignore. Knowing how uncomfortable this can be, we tend to avoid prayer or make it a one-way religious recitation. We'll do just about anything rather than sit quietly in His presence and admit that we're hurt.

If this describes you, let me warn you that when you hide pain, you're handing Satan a weapon to use against you. He's the one who keeps telling you to not admit the hurt. He wants you to believe that being honest with God will make you weak. But that's a lie. Silence only serves to reinforce the walls raised around your life. And the problem with walls is that they not only keep out the bad but keep out the good, making you unable to receive all God has for you.

Please know there's no wound God can't heal, no pain He can't remove, and no sorrow He can't resolve. With God, all things are possible (Matthew 19:26)! But first, we must be honest. David's honesty was the first step to receiving his healing, and it's your first step too.

2. Worship God and refuse despair.

If David were here, I believe he'd tell you, "The best way to get back on your *feet* is to get on your *knees* in worship."

Another temptation in the wake of pain is to turn away from God and turn to despair. Despair is a darkness that invades our soul when we turn inward and dwell on our hurt, thinking about it again and again until we have no hope. Although disappointments are inevitable, despair is a choice. When your life has fallen to pieces, you can focus on the pain, which causes greater despair, or you can focus on God. The antidote for despair is worship, because when we worship, we focus on God's goodness.

Often, we forget how great God is because we fixate on our circumstances and let them dictate whether and how we worship. *Circumstances* change, but the *character of God* never changes. Our situation may look bad, but God is never bad. He's always good! He never lies, He never leaves, and He never fails. God is worthy of praise regardless of our circumstances. Let your worship be based on your amazing God, not on your circumstances or the kind of week you're having.

Now, you may say, "But my life is in pieces. Nothing is good." Even if everything in your life appears bad, if you look hard enough, you'll discover the goodness of God. Just focus on every good thing you can think of, like the fact that you have breath in your lungs and a heartbeat in your chest. Most importantly, realize that God still loves you, He still cares about you, He still has a plan for you, and He's still working to put you back together.

Choosing to worship will also remind you that because you're God's child, you'll spend eternity with Him in heaven, where there's no pain, loss, disease, depression, rejection, fear, unemployment, abuse, or addiction. Everything wrong in this world will be right in the next, and you'll spend trillions more years there than here.

The fact is despair and worship can't coexist in the same heart. When you gaze on God and the truth that He is your eternal hope, perfect provider, wonderful counselor, able protector, and unfailing friend, there's no way you can stay hopeless.

I know worshiping God when you're overwhelmed and hurting may seem odd, but it's the answer.

3. Surrender your future to God.

In loss, one of the most challenging tasks is to move forward. That's because we don't know what the future will look like. It's unknown, and you can't know how everything will work out. But you can still move forward by surrendering your future to God and trusting Him to work it out.

That's what David did when he basically said, "I can't bring my child back, so I'll look to the future when I can go to be with him." That was his way of saying, "I'm going to trust God to work this out." That's also the sentiment of Romans 8:28: "We know that in all things God works for the good of those who love him, who have been called according to his purpose."

Now, while Romans 8:28 is certainly one of the most encouraging Scripture verses, it's also one of the most misunderstood. First, notice it doesn't say everything that happens is good. There's a lot of bad in the world, like racism, disease, abuse, disasters, and terrorism. But God's promise is to take everything—including the bad—and work it for our good.

Let me illustrate. I wasn't a coffee drinker a few years ago, but having five kids has made me caffeine dependent. When I get up in the morning and take that first sip, all I can say is, "Man, that's good!"

Of course, I'm not saying the mug is good or the hot water is good or the filter is good. I'm not even saying the coffee grounds are good. If I were to chew on the filter or eat the coffee grounds, it would taste very bad. Individually, none of those ingredients are good. But at some point in history, a master designer figured out how to take hot water, paper filters, and coffee beans and work them together until they became good.

In life, not everything is *God-sent*, but everything is *God-used*. Your past and present may not be good, but you have a Master Designer who knows how to take all the bad, all the pain, and all the unjust treatment and work it until it becomes something good in your life. So be encouraged! In the middle of your worst day, God is at work. In the middle of your most stressful moments, God is at work. And in the middle of your hopelessness, God is at work.

> *In life, not everything is God-sent, but everything is God-used.*

Even though you can't see it, feel it, or understand it, God is at work because He promised He would. He's never left a promise unfulfilled, and He won't start with you. I know it may seem like this struggle will be the story of your life, but it's not. Better days are ahead, and you can live with hope because God is up to something good.

All that said, I need to draw your attention to the fact that the promise of Romans 8:28 isn't for everyone. It's only for those who are "called according to His purpose." This means you must surrender your life to God for Him to bring about His good purpose.

Think again about David. Because he surrendered his future to God, God took his sins of adultery, lying, and murder—along with the loss of his child—and worked it all into a new marriage that birthed Solomon, who became the wisest, most accomplished king in Israel's history. Centuries later, through this same family line, the greatest King of all time was born—King Jesus! Indeed, God will work all things together for good in your life if you surrender yourself to Him.

4. *Take it one day at a time.*

I love how the Bible details the small steps David took after the tragic loss of his child. It says he got up, took a bath, ate something, and consoled his wife. In essence, he took one step at a time, one day at a time.

What step do you need to take right now? Maybe you need to be willing to connect with people again. Or maybe you need to begin reading your Bible or set an appointment with a counselor or ask someone for prayer. You might think, *Well, that's not much of a step,* but a limp is still a step forward when it's in the right direction.

Some time ago, Kayla and I were traveling and decided to take a detour to visit my grandmother. Now, I have to confess I love my grandmother and I wanted to see her, but I also love her pecan pie. And after eating a piece or three, we sat on her back porch and I asked her about her life. She told us about her childhood, her first job at a movie theater, and how she met my grandfather. But then she told us about a season that could only be described as tragic.

First, she described the night the state police called and told her a man in her hometown had gone mad and murdered her parents in a rampage. She then told us about the Sunday evening she was in church and an electrical fire started in her home. By the time she arrived, nothing was left but a pile of smoldering ash. Finally, she shared about the time my grandfather was diagnosed with cancer. Though he fought the disease valiantly, he died at the age of fifty-six. The greatest shock for us came when she said all these tragic events happened within the span of eighteen months.

Now, if you visited my grandmother, she'd welcome you in, give you a big hug, offer you a piece of pie, and then tell you how much she loves God. Nearly every time I'm with her she'll tear up and say, "God has just been so good to me." But after this conversation, I couldn't quite grasp how she could be so kind, generous, loving, and selfless.

So I asked her, "How did you make it through so many terrible situations and keep your faith?" And she said, "Honey, me and Jesus just took it a day at a time."

Both her life and David's tell me you're going to make it! You won't be frozen by fear. You won't grow bitter with hate. And you won't have a breakdown and quit. You'll laugh again, love again, and see God's best in your life. And you'll live with hope, because you and Jesus will take it one day at a time. Each day, He'll be there to help you take another step, and step by step, day by day, piece by piece, He'll put you back together. He'll build a new dream and piece together a new promise, and somehow, through it all, you'll be better than you are today.

Heavenly Father, You know my heart and all I've been through. At times it feels as though I'll never be able to move past my pain. But I'm surrendering it to You. And despite my circumstances being far from where I'd like them to be, I'm deciding to worship You for who You are. Amen.

3

The Risk of Remaining Hurt

Are you a risk taker?

Recently, I read an article listing risks you should intentionally take before turning forty. It made me laugh, because I thought about the difference between what those under forty and those over forty define as a risk. For instance, for those under forty, a risk is white water rafting, skydiving, or hiking the Grand Canyon. For those over forty, a risk is exercising without stretching first, eating Taco Bell far too late in the evening, or sleeping without a Posturepedic pillow!

Whether you're a risk taker or someone who plays it safe, you need to know there's great risk in remaining hurt. Your emotional health can be the greatest limitation to God's plan for your life. If you have a clean, healthy heart, He can do anything through you. But if your heart is tainted or hardened by hurt, His plan is limited. After all, how can a God who is love use someone whose heart is unable to love?

This is why some people keep growing while others never reach their full potential. Everyone experiences emotional wounds, and at some point, God moves to address those unhealed places. Growing

43

people welcome and cooperate with God's work in their lives, but some people resist Him and settle for being partially healed.

But God isn't OK with partial healing. Jesus gave His whole life so we could be made whole. This is why the Holy Spirit relentlessly persists in confronting our toxic emotions, opening our unhealed memories, and removing layers of pride.

Paul's Advice about Holding On to Pain

You might not think holding on to pain is a big deal, but it could derail your God-given destiny. And I believe this is why the apostle Paul chose to warn his young apprentice Timothy about church hurt in his final letter.

Timothy was serving as the pastor of the church at Ephesus, and like you, he'd been transformed by the message of Jesus and now had one thing on his mind—living out God's will. Knowing this, Paul highlighted some essentials for fulfilling God's will that include how to deal with fear, maintain focus, and aim to finish well.

Toward the end of his advice, seemingly out of nowhere, Paul brought up a man named Alexander: "Alexander the metalworker did me a great deal of harm. The Lord will repay him for what he has done. You too should be on your guard against him" (2 Timothy 4:14–15).

A casual reading of this passage would likely give you the idea that this shout-out was out of place. But considering his mentoring heart, I believe Paul was saying, "Timothy, as you follow God's plan, you'll cross paths with hurtful people who can cause great pain. Guard against them, know that God will address any wrong, but don't let the pain linger."

We might think holding some resentment is the cost of doing business in a broken world. Or that everyone has an "Alexander" in their life, and therefore we all carry a measure of anger or pain. But Paul knew holding on to pain is a liability, because unbeknownst to many of us, it causes us to abandon God's plan and begin walking in the enemy's plan. For Paul, nothing was more important than releasing pain, because it frees us to carry out God's plan.

In your own pursuit of God's will, at some point you've probably been wounded by someone in the church. And whatever took place, it caused you a level of pain. The question is, Does the pain remain?

Who's Really Behind the Pain

At this point in our journey, I must press "pause" to address something vital. In order for you to gain insight from Paul's letter and the principles I'm sharing, you must come into agreement with what the Bible says about evil.

We know evil exists; we just don't like to think about it. Yet according to Scripture, behind every evil person and evil act lurks the real enemy of the soul—Satan. He works from the spiritual realm and is 100 percent evil and 100 percent relentless in his pursuit. Whether or not you want to be, you're in a spiritual battle against enemy forces.

One of Satan's greatest strategies is to deceive people into thinking he doesn't exist. It's popular to imagine him as a cartoon character dressed in red with a long tail, holding a pitchfork, and with horns on his head. This thinking is so prevalent that Barna Research discovered that 60 percent of Christians believe the devil and demons are symbolic, not literal.[1] This belief carries major consequences.

Jesus Himself identified Satan as our adversary, telling us He saw Satan fall from heaven with His own two eyes (Luke 10:18). Both Matthew 4 and Luke 4 detail how Satan tempted Jesus in the desert and Jesus emerged victorious after forty days. Jesus also encountered numerous demons and cast them out of people by the power of His word. Peter, Paul, and John all wrote about a literal enemy. In fact, the word *demon* appears eighty-two times in the New Kings James Version of the Bible—sixty-one times in the Gospels alone.

For a person to believe Satan and demons aren't real is to disbelieve and disagree with Jesus and all the apostles.

The enemy loves nothing more than our denial that he exists because it allows him to work covertly. Ask yourself who wins in the game of church hurt. Leaders don't win. Victims don't win. And faith communities don't win. The only one who celebrates our pain is our spiritual enemy.

With that in mind, Paul refused to be subtle in his letter to Timothy. Instead, he clearly exposed our spiritual enemy as the one behind every wrong trying to exploit our wounds. To foil Satan's plans, Paul told his ministry protégé and us:

> The Lord's servant must not be quarrelsome but must be kind to everyone, able to teach, not resentful. Opponents must be gently instructed, in the hope that God will grant them repentance leading them to a knowledge of the truth, and that they will come to their senses and escape from the trap of the devil, who has taken them captive to do his will.
>
> 2 Timothy 2:24–26

The first rule of any battle is to know your enemy. In this passage, Paul provides a major intelligence briefing. First, he reveals that resentment or untreated pain is the open door the enemy uses to enter our lives. Second, Paul discloses that our spiritual enemy's goal is to take us captive and turn us into pawns to do his will.

The Enemy's Playbook for Your Pain

The moment you were wounded, Satan started his work to take you captive. And if given enough time, he'll deceptively lead you through a process that turns your pain into chains that place you under his control. But you can't overcome a process you can't identify.

With that said, allow me to explain four steps the enemy hopes to take to pull you under his control:

1. *Trapping you with an offense*

The one thing certain about all relationships is that sooner or later you'll probably be hurt. But in the moments that follow someone's mistreating you—whether intentional or not—you can choose to either *overlook it* or *be offended by it*. To overlook it means putting it out of your mind, whereas to be offended means giving what the person did mental space for a prolonged period.

Today too many people are easily offended because they don't realize how deadly this trap can be. The Greek word for offense is *scandalon*. It's the same word used to describe the part of an animal trap that holds the bait. If you've ever watched Looney Toons, you've probably seen Wile E. Coyote set a round, jagged-edged trap for his nemesis, Road Runner. In the middle of that trap is a small plate where he places birdseed as bait. That plate—or trigger—is a picture of the word *scandalon*.

So when the Holy Spirit chose that word to explain offense, he was giving us a warning: to take an offense is to take the bait of a trap that's been set for us.

The thing about traps is that they use different bait, and our spiritual enemy has studied us to determine what bait works best. He knows some value loyalty, and therefore he baits them with betrayal. He knows others value kindness, and that's why he baits them with harsh words. He sets the bait in hopes we'll take it. If we do, we give him a place in our mental space to operate, and that enables him to move us closer to his control. Offense is a snare of which we must be aware and avoid.

2. *Poisoning your perspective*

Once the bait is taken, it begins to consume our minds. We rehearse what happened again and again, unaware that every replay is releasing spiritual toxins into our soul.

God warns us about this process in Hebrews 12:15: "Let no one become like a bitter plant that grows up and causes many troubles

47

with its poison" (GNT). The Greek word for poison here means "to dye." Every time you replay the hurt in your mind, the poison of offense spreads and colors how you see the world. It becomes the filter for how you see other people, future events, and even your heavenly Father. This is the point at which offense mutates into anger and opens the door to the devil.

3. *Slipping through a door open to evil influence*

Though you would never intentionally show hospitality to your spiritual enemy, when you allow anger to go unaddressed, you're putting a "welcome mat" for him at the door of your heart. This is clearly stated in Ephesians 4:26–27, where Paul wrote, "Don't let anger control you or be fuel for revenge, not for even a day. Don't give the slanderous accuser, the Devil, an opportunity to manipulate you!" (TPT).

The Greek word for opportunity paints the picture of a strategic place—maybe from a high vantage point—from where a general would want to conduct battle. This explains why when you're hurt, your thoughts race out of control, your emotions are aggravated, and you have no peace. The enemy has assumed a strategic place of influence in your mind, where he intends to direct your steps like a general directs his troops.

4. *Making you his operative*

This was the enemy's goal the entire time. His trap was designed not only to damage you but to take you captive so you could be used to damage others. That's why hurt people hurt people: the enemy's plan is to multiply pain through offense.

I know this may be hard to grasp because we picture being an operative of the enemy as a scene from a horror movie. But the power of unaddressed pain is so great that it can turn the most dedicated follower of Jesus into an enemy of God's will. And I'll prove it through Scripture.

Judas's Betrayal Displays Satan's Playbook

In Matthew 26, we find Jesus and His twelve disciples in a house when a woman enters with an expensive perfume. After making her way to Jesus' feet, she breaks open the container and pours the perfume on him as an act of worship.

This extravagant act stuns the disciples. John's account of the event says Judas (who served as Jesus' accountant) publicly chastises the woman for her misuse of funds. When Jesus hears this, He publicly chastises Judas for expressing greed and not recognizing this woman's worship. Dumbfounded by Jesus' decision to side with this woman over him, a dedicated follower, Judas is deeply offended.

I believe Judas, once ensnared by the enemy, sat quietly fuming through the rest of the dinner. The longer he sat in the sweet aroma of that perfume, the more the poison of offense spread in his soul. As he watched this woman interact with Jesus, anger opened the door of his heart, giving the enemy's voice a position to influence his thoughts.

The Bible says immediately following the dinner:

> One of the Twelve—the one called Judas Iscariot—went to the chief priests and asked, "What are you willing to give me if I deliver [Jesus] over to you?" So they counted out for him thirty pieces of silver. From then on Judas watched for an opportunity to hand him over.
>
> Matthew 26:14–16

How powerful is unaddressed pain? It caused one of Jesus' disciples to become one of the enemy's destroyers.

Don't for a minute think this couldn't happen in your life. Pain has caused many a person to slander others, seek revenge, run to an addiction, resign a position, or abandon their faith. Whose will is being accomplished in each of these acts? Certainly not God's! Yet this is the risk of allowing pain to remain. It causes you to abandon God's will and begin doing the enemy's bidding.

Realize that both God and the enemy have a plan for your life, and what you do with your pain determines whose plan you'll walk in.

A Snare I Know Too Well

One of the most pivotal years of my life was the year I became a lead pastor. And during that time I believe the enemy tried to highjack God's will through church hurt I endured.

With any change in leadership, people are unsettled and make their opinions known. In this case, I was following a great leader who'd served the church for nearly thirty years, so it was reasonable for people to question my ability to lead such a large church.

But one person abandoned all reason and made it a mission to ensure I didn't fill that position. I'm still not sure why, but in the months leading up to my installation, the goal seemed to be making my life a living hell. For example, attempts to discredit me to the elders of the church, gathering others to "enlighten them" about projected missteps the church was making, an email to leaders questioning my qualifications, attacking my integrity, and demanding my resignation.

What made the situation especially hard was that there was never an attempt to discuss any of this face-to-face. The attacks all came from behind a screen. I was already battling feelings of inadequacy, and these words and actions served as reinforcements for those defeating thoughts.

To say I was offended would be an understatement. I had taken the bait hook, line, and sinker. I thought about the situation constantly, and my emotions quickly turned to anger. I must have reread those demeaning emails a dozen times, and each time I did, the poison flowed further through my soul. My guard was down, and my heart was wide open for the enemy to take his position of influence. The attitudes I displayed and the words I said during that season sounded exactly like the devil.

One day on a prayer walk, I was explaining to God all He should do to this individual (striking with leprosy was just the tip of the iceberg). I went on and on, until as an act of mercy, God let me hear myself talking. For maybe the first time, I heard the bitterness in my words and immediately had the epiphany that I sounded nothing like Jesus. I realized our church was about to get a pastor being influenced by Satan, not by the Holy Spirit!

That season taught me several lessons, but the most impactful was that God can undo anything the enemy has done. Through His grace, God has designed a way for us to disable the enemy's trap. It's called *forgiveness*. If you've been hurt and happen to find yourself in the same condition I was in, I want you to know you can choose to take back control by forgiving the person who wronged you.

I realize that might seem impossible from where you are right now, but one of the reasons is that forgiveness may be the most misunderstood concept in all of Scripture. For instance, forgiving an offense—releasing it—doesn't require restoration, and it doesn't mean the wrong is completely forgotten. It simply means repeatedly deciding not to dwell on what the person did or hold them in hate.

The Process of Forgiveness

That said, I'll take the remainder of this chapter to walk you through each of the three steps in the process.

1. Ask God for help.

When they're hurt, one of the biggest mistakes people make is trying to forgive in their own strength. But forgiveness isn't natural; it's supernatural. It's a divine act of God's Spirit in your heart. Therefore, forgiveness starts with prayer. Choosing to go to God in prayer before focusing on the person who hurt you is critical because it provides the Holy Spirit the opportunity to remind you of two things about God.

First, God understands. You've never had a wound with which Jesus didn't empathize. He uniquely endured physical, emotional, mental, and spiritual hurt, including severe mistreatment from the religious community. The Bible says, "He came to His own, and His own did not receive Him" (John 1:11 NKJV). It never ceases to amaze me that the most vicious lies and the ultimate rejection of Jesus came not from the Greeks, the Romans, or the pagans. It came from those who were considered children of God. Know for certain that God understands what you're going through.

Forgiveness isn't natural; it's supernatural. It's a divine act of God's Spirit in your heart.

Second, God is just. Occasionally, my kids fight (and by occasionally, I mean minute by minute). As their father, it's my job to ensure each offense is addressed justly. The problem is I rarely see the wrongs committed or know exactly what happened. This leaves me in the impossible position of needing to determine whose claim is true. After I intently listen to both sides and try to read their faces, I put my best guess forward to bring about a just result.

Thankfully, our heavenly Father doesn't have to guess about your pain. He knows exactly what happened in your situation. He knows who wronged you, how and when they did it, and the pain it's caused. This is significant, because it means you don't have to keep hold of resentment to prove what they did. God knows and has promised to personally make it right. That's why Paul had confidence that God would deal with Alexander, who did him wrong (2 Timothy 4:14). Everything done in the dark will be brought into the light, and justice will be served.

2. Admit you're offended.

Imagine you're sitting in an exam room, and the doctor walks in and immediately notices your fever, coughing, and labored breathing. She looks at you and says, "How long have you been sick?" And you respond by saying, "Sick? Oh, I'm not sick. I feel great!" You'd be referred to a psychiatrist!

Similarly, few people openly admit they're offended. I think part of the problem is that saying we're "bitter" or "resentful" seems extreme, and no one wants to own those labels. Another problem is we rationalize or minimize our offense, saying to ourselves, *I'm just frustrated, not full-blown bitter.* We can label it any way we want, but until we honestly admit we're offended, we won't receive any relief.

This means you must be specific about the source of your offense. Sometimes we carry anger so long we forget the details that surround it, which is why we need the Holy Spirit's help to call to our remembrance what exactly happened.

In Scripture, forgiveness is always referred to in accounting terms, and correct accounting requires exact numbers and specific formulas to get the right result. Likewise, forgiveness requires you to name the person who offended you and their exact action so you can get the right result.

So who hurt you? When did it happen? What do you feel they owe you? Take your time to accurately answer these questions. You can't offer forgiveness for something you haven't specified.

3. Act in obedience.

The single most common misconception about forgiveness might be that it will occur with time or that you'll eventually "feel" like forgiving. But Scripture never presents forgiveness as a random occurrence; it's always an act of obedience we choose. Consider Ephesians 4:31–32: "Get rid of all bitterness, rage and anger, brawling and slander, along with every form of malice. Be kind and compassionate to one another, forgiving each other, just as in Christ God forgave you."

In essence, Paul is saying, "I'm not asking you to feel it; I'm asking you to do it." I wish there was a switch God could flip in your heart, but forgiveness isn't something Jesus can do for you. Yes, His finished work on the cross cleansed you of all your sins because you couldn't do that for yourself, but Jesus can't forgive your coworker, ex-spouse, or former pastor for you. You must make that choice on your own.

What Does It Look Like to Forgive?

First, decide your offender owes you nothing. They don't owe you an explanation, an apology, or a repayment. Let me be clear once more. Releasing them of their offense does not require restoration. It simply means repeatedly deciding not to dwell on what they did or hold them in hate.

Most people never forgive because they're waiting to *feel* like forgiving. But you won't feel your way into forgiveness. It requires an intentional decision. And that decision is demonstrated by choosing to pray for the person who wronged you—and as many times as you need to. Jesus tells us this in Luke 6:28: "Bless those who curse you. Pray for those who hurt you" (NLT). Basically, to bless those who curse you means to pray for them what you pray for yourself.

Therefore, to forgive requires an intentional decision to forgive your offender and drop the mental and emotional charges you've been holding against them. It also requires purposely blessing them with your prayers. Eventually, what you've decided in your mind will begin to affect your heart, because blessing forces forgiveness out of your head into your heart.

Let me warn you: forgiveness isn't a one-time event; it's a daily exercise. Every time you remember how someone hurt you, you'll have to decide to release it and forgive them. And you'll know when you've totally released a person's offense when your pain has been replaced with peace.

Forgiveness isn't a one-time event; it's a daily exercise.

Finally, anticipate God's goodness. When you choose to forgive, it will feel as though a weight has lifted. You'll regain joy and experience a fresh connection to God. Equally important, forgiveness will make a way for God's purpose to prevail in your life once again.

Years ago, I had to walk out this process myself. I asked God for help, decided mentally to release what I felt owed, and then prayed for the man who hurt me for what seemed like a thousand times.

Eventually, though, peace returned, the enemy's voice was silenced, and I was able to move forward.

Then one Sunday years later, I was on the platform speaking when out in the crowd I saw the man who'd caused all that pain. What happened replayed in my mind, but instead of feeling anger or pain, I felt compassion, which mirrored God's heart. The feeling was so strong that as soon as the service was over, I stepped to the lobby to extend him a welcome invitation to our church anytime.

God's ability to heal is greater than the enemy's ability to destroy. What was done to you was wrong, but God is so creative and capable that He can weave it into His purpose for your life.

That day reminded me that my purpose could have ended because of my pain. I'm so grateful I allowed God to address my hurt and remove the enemy's influence. That experience taught me that the person who gains the most from forgiveness is the one who does the forgiving.

Because a fresh season is just around the corner, the Holy Spirit wants to address what's in your heart. Don't risk missing it. Allow Him to reveal and heal the hurt that's been concealed.

God, thank You for opening my eyes to the enemy's plan to steal, kill, and destroy. In this moment, I admit I have unresolved pain and I'm holding a measure of resentment. Though it goes against everything I feel, help me release and bless those who caused this pain. In Jesus' name, amen.

✝

PART TWO

Finding God's Path to Healing

4

Hypocrisy

I recently read about a collection of gym franchises that tried a new strategy to enhance their clientele's experience. It was called Pizza Monday, and it gave members free pizza. Can you imagine driving by your local gym, looking through the window, and seeing people on a treadmill downing a slice? My guess is you'd do a double take because you'd think, *What kind of place pushes exercise* and *an extra-large with cheese?*

That's a similar sentiment many have when they look at some people inside the church. They're confused by:

- the guy in small group who talked about loving Jesus but, it turns out, had been having an affair.
- the student who posts Scripture but, it turns out, cheated on tests.
- the boss who talks spiritually but treats employees horribly.
- the friend who appears so godly yet gossips uncontrollably.

Let me be clear. Hypocrisy is not when someone makes a mistake —that's being human. Every one of us has said or done things we wish we hadn't, and we're all in the process of being shaped into the image of Christ. Hypocrisy is when we claim to be one thing but consistently live contrary to it. It's when our public persona is different from our private character—and we're okay with it.

Now, just like church hurt in general, hypocrisy isn't a new problem for the church; it's been around since it began. As a matter of fact, the first sin recorded in the early church dealt with hypocrisy. Isn't it interesting that the enemy's initial strategy of attack wasn't through bad theology or conflict? His first attempt was to get church people to claim to be one way while they lived another way. He knows the widespread damage hypocrisy causes.

Brennan Manning, author of *The Ragamuffin Gospel*, said,

> The greatest single cause of atheism in the world today is Christians, who acknowledge Jesus with their lips, then walk out the door, and deny Him with their lifestyle. That is what an unbelieving world simply finds unbelievable.[1]

A careful study of Scripture reveals that Manning was right, and I can prove it by showing you how seriously God dealt with hypocrisy in the early church.

Hypocrisy: The Early Church's First Crisis

In Acts 4, Jesus had already ascended into heaven, the disciples were in charge, and the early church was thriving. God was using ordinary people to do extraordinary things. For example, a man named Barnabas, operating in the gift of giving, chose to sell a field and then donate all the proceeds to the church so more people could receive ministry (Acts 4:36–37). Many took notice of Barnabas's incredible generosity, and it launched him into a greater position of leadership.

But this is where the story takes a dark turn. Scripture says two of the people who noticed what Barnabas did were Ananias and his wife, Sapphira. Like Barnabas, they, too, sold property. But for some reason, they said they were giving all the proceeds while withholding a portion for themselves. They portrayed one thing publicly while doing something else privately:

> There was a certain man named Ananias who, with his wife, Sapphira, sold some property. He brought part of the money to the apostles, claiming it was the full amount. With his wife's consent, he kept the rest. Then Peter said, "Ananias, why have you let Satan fill your heart? You lied to the Holy Spirit, and you kept some of the money for yourself. The property was yours to sell or not sell, as you wished. And after selling it, the money was also yours to give away. How could you do a thing like this? You weren't lying to us but to God!" As soon as Ananias heard these words, he fell to the floor and died.
>
> Acts 5:1–5 NLT

When Sapphira returned, she lied as well, claiming they gave all the proceeds from the sale to the church. And her fate was the same as her husband's. She fell dead, and they took her out and buried her.

Can you imagine if something like that happened today?

A small group leader calls and says, "Jim, you coming to group tonight?"

"Yeah, I'll be there."

But when Jim hangs up, his wife says, "I thought you weren't going,"

"I'm not. I just didn't want to disappoint him."

Then boom! Jim's dead. I think that would cause people to think twice before casually claiming something that isn't true.

Although the Lord's response to Ananias and Sapphira seems harsh for such a merciful God, He had a purpose for it, and we find it in Acts 5:11: "Great fear gripped the entire church and everyone else who heard what had happened" (NLT). Turns out, God wanted His followers to be scared to death of hypocrisy.

Faith at Face Value

If it seems like authenticity is in decline and pretending has become a cultural norm, you're right. We're no longer surprised by moral and ethical scandals, and we've become comfortable with partial truths. But regardless of what people think and what's trending, integrity still matters to God. He's not looking for perfection, but He won't tolerate facades because He knows the damage hypocrisy does:

- It destroys the reputation of a church.
- It damages the unity of marriages.
- It ruins the standing of businesses.
- It births resentment in our children.
- It's deadly to our spiritual life.

God has called us to live a *holy life*. Now, you may think that means keeping to a long list of rules or dressing a certain way, but it doesn't. It's simply doing our best to live authentically as we pursue Jesus each day.

The fact is every one of us has two lives—a seen life and an unseen life. Holiness is when both are integrated and there's no difference between what we profess and what we practice. Think of it this way: *holiness* is when our life is *wholly* God's. When that's the case, we can live with the peace of God, knowing nothing is hidden. We can live out the calling of God, empowered by His Spirit. And we can expect the blessing of God because our life is pleasing to Him.

Having a faith people can take at face value means we need to come to grips with two inescapable truths.

We've All Been Hurt by Hypocrisy

Years ago, a friend of mine shared about his life before Christ with me. Held captive by gambling and alcohol, Casey ended up cheating on his wife, getting divorced, and eventually hitting rock bottom. With nowhere else to go, he moved in with his mother, but she had a stipulation—he had to join her for church.

Surprisingly, Casey enjoyed the services and even made some new friends. Things were looking up—until one day someone introduced him to a couple of the church members. But no introduction was needed. They were two of the people he'd partied with. On Fridays they acted like frat boys and on Sunday choir boys. As you might imagine, Casey was angry, confused, and crushed by their hypocrisy.

Maybe you've felt the same disappointment Casey did. Most of us have. If so, you need to know that disappointment left untreated becomes disenfranchisement. This may be why you carry a suspicion or distrust of others and shut down and refuse to open up to anyone. Consequently, you've become spiritually stuck. You want to follow Jesus, but you don't want to engage with His people. If that describes your current condition, however, there's hope.

Jesus Is Your Great Physician

If you've been struggling in your faith, unresolved disappointment may be the root cause. Left unchecked, disappointment can disable and damage your heart, allowing apathy in your faith and fear for your future. Having said this, I have bad news and good news.

The bad news is your heart won't recover on its own, and no pill or prayer will fix it. You need spiritual heart surgery. The good news is the only physician who can successfully perform the surgery is willing to take you on as a patient. His name is Jesus, and He specializes in mending hearts broken by disappointment. That's what He announced in Luke 4:18: "[God] has sent Me to heal the brokenhearted" (NKJV).

As someone who's endured many disappointments but made a full recovery, I can tell you you're in great hands with Jesus. His bedside manner is the best. He's always peaceful, always kind, and always loving. He's so patient that He'll stay with you for as long as it takes. And by His nail scars, you know He understands your hurt.

Additionally, Jesus' skills are second to none. His eyes can see in the darkest corners of your heart, and His hands can handle your deepest hurts. His Word is like a scalpel that removes the infectious lies of the enemy. His resurrection power ensures He's never lost a patient. And you don't have to worry about obtaining an appointment—He's always available.

Furthermore, coverage isn't an issue because He covered the cost on the cross. There's no condition He cannot heal and no heart He cannot revive—and that's why He's called the Great Physician!

The only requirement is for you to consent to His work by surrendering your disappointment. Don't let someone else's dysfunction become the reason for your faith decline.

Recovery and Recalibration

I've done some deep study and discovered why church hurt exists (are you ready?). It exists because churches are made up of people, and people are messed up! Too often we forget people are all made in God's image but also have a fallen nature. So the reason church hurt hurts so much is that when we're worshiping with someone, it's easy to forget they can wound us. So examining your expectations of others is vital to experience healing.

Over the years, I've learned that frustration is often the result of my expectations of others being too high. It seems we have the greatest expectations for those we're closest to, and the greater the expectations we have, the greater the chance we'll be offended by them at some point.

One of the things I love about God is that He's honest about human nature. Psalm 103:14 says, "He knows how weak we are" (NLT). God is never frustrated with you because His expectations of you are never unreasonable. He knows how weak you are!

As we allow God to shape our perspective of people, He recalibrates our expectations so they're realistic. If we ask, He'll help us:

- *See people appropriately.* Isn't it funny how when we look at the faults in others, we quickly attribute them to their flawed character, but when we look at our own flaws, we attribute them to the tremendous challenges we've faced? God levels the playing field and enables us to see others as He does and give them the same grace we ourselves need.

- *See God appropriately.* Often, our high expectations of others reveal we're looking to them for something only God can provide. Your spouse can't satisfy your soul; only God can do that. Likewise, your boss can't make your dreams true; only God can do that. Moreover, your pastor can't transform your situation; only God can. The only one who's completely selfless, flawless, and faithful is God! Although He does work through people, God is our Source and the first one we should turn to for anything.

Returning to God's call for you will also help you heal from the wound of hypocrisy. When we allow the hypocritical actions of others to stifle our relationship with God and His purpose for our lives, we've placed too much power in their hands. I'm not trivializing your trauma, but why should we miss out on God's best because someone else was at their worst? It doesn't make sense!

The apostle Paul consistently encountered people who claimed to live for God yet acted like the devil. When he faced this kind of opposition, he shook the dust off his feet as a warning to them and went to the next town (Acts 13:51). He didn't argue (or post about those who treated him poorly on social media). He simply shook off the "dirt" trying to cling to him and set out for his next ministry opportunity.

> *Sometimes the most spiritual thing you can do is shake off your disappointment and get back to what God has called you to do.*

Sometimes the most spiritual thing you can do is shake off your disappointment and get back to what God has called you to do. If someone has done you wrong, ask God to empower you to shake it off and get back to feeding your faith. God can and will work in your life regardless of what others are doing. Don't let someone's inconsistency impair what God wants to do in and through you.

We've All Been Guilty of Hypocrisy

Unlike some of the other wounds we'll cover in this book, hypocrisy is unique because we're all victims and perpetrators at the same time. In most cases we didn't aim to live a double life, but we must accept our actions still caused damage.

I personally know the struggle of living with a gap between my private and public life. One of my greatest mistakes was trying to live out my purpose before God had matured my character. It happened when I first began my ministry journey. I was on staff at a church, but I was still struggling with attitudes and habits below the standard a minister should hold. To look the part, though, I hid my struggles. Instead of coming clean and asking for help, like I encouraged others to do, I kept my issues secret and acted as though they didn't exist.

Then one night when I was in a worship service, a guest speaker said something that changed the trajectory of my life. As he was closing, he suddenly stopped and said, "A minister here is living a secret life. Everyone thinks you have it all together, but you don't. If you don't stop living with compromise, you'll void the destiny God has for you."

I felt as though a spotlight from heaven was shining on me, because I knew he was talking to me. And that night a great reverence for God was restored to me. The Bible calls it *the fear of the Lord*, and as I received this empowerment, I was able to take the steps necessary to live free and honestly.

Regardless of why, when honesty *stops*, hypocrisy *starts*. If you're living a double life—acting one way in public and another way in private—there's a pathway to freedom. And it starts with realizing nothing is hidden from God. Hebrews 4:13 tells us, "Nothing in all creation is hidden from God's sight. Everything is uncovered and laid bare before the eyes of him to whom we must give account." God knows us inside and out. He's aware of every thought, motive, and action. He knows our habits, our strengths, and our weaknesses. He even knows our thoughts before we think them and our words before we speak them.

So don't for one minute think you're the exception, the one person who can outwit God. Although you may be able to hide things from people, you can't hide anything from Him. Yet despite your sin, He still loves you unconditionally! As long as you keep a secret life, you put your destiny in jeopardy. God will never bless who you pretend to be, but He will greatly bless who He created you to be.

You can regain your strength by coming clean with God. Years back, *TIME* magazine did a story on a service that allowed anyone to call and get something off their chest for a fee. This company received confessions of everything from marital infidelity to murder, and on average they received up to ten thousand calls a day.[2] Why would people pay to confess? Because the human heart wasn't meant to carry the weight of secrets.

Hypocrites have heavy souls because living a fake life is exhausting. Many in that state attempt to medicate, escape, and justify their actions, but the only way to find lasting relief and regain their strength is through confession. God's Word says, "If we confess our sins, he is faithful and just and will forgive us our sins and purify us from all unrighteousness" (1 John 1:9).

To confess your sins to God is to humble yourself and admit your weaknesses and where you've missed the mark. Confession opens a channel for God's strength to flow into your life again. If you've been avoiding this practice because you think God will be angry if you ask Him to forgive you for something you've done numerous times, be at peace. He's not looking for perfection, just honesty. Remember, He already knows about your ongoing struggle, so just be real, tell

Him how you feel, and ask Him to forgive you and strengthen you to overcome the temptation altogether.

Healing also comes from being honest with others. James 5:16 says, "Confess your sins to each other and pray for each other so that you may be healed." Notice we confess our sins to God for *forgiveness* (1 John 1:9), but we confess to others for *healing*. I wonder how many people have been forgiven but not healed.

To be clear, I'm not encouraging you to broadcast your issues. The person you confess to should be someone you trust and feel safe with. This could be a mentor, a long-time friend, or even a small group you know will keep what you say confidential. If someone broke your confidence in the past, don't let that keep you from opening up to someone else and experiencing the healing you need.

I know fear is fighting against every inclination you have toward coming clean, but refuse to return to hiding. Remember, hypocrisy is deadly. It kills marriages, families, churches, and your faith. On the other hand, authenticity receives God's grace, brings life, and attracts the attention of those looking for truth.

I encourage you to set a time to talk to someone soon. Remember, the secret you want to conceal most is the one you most need to reveal. There is strength on the other side of your obedience.

Finally, if you find yourself reeling from the discovery that someone isn't who you thought they were, refuse a cynical outlook and ask God to give you discernment concerning the people in your life. I believe He will guide you to set up healthy boundaries with some while at the same time guide you to invest deeper in those striving to live an authentic Christian life.

God, the frustration and disappointment I carry is so strong, but in this moment I release it to You. Help me shake off what happened and refocus on what You have for me. Additionally, search my heart and reveal any inauthenticity in me. I want to live holy and help end this problem. Amen.

5

Judgmentalism

Tessa and her husband were excited to have moved back to the Midwest. And she was thrilled to have a new job at a local church because she'd always wanted to help people. This opportunity was a dream come true, and her first two months couldn't have gone better.

Then one day she was eating lunch with a small group of coworkers when someone asked about her life before Christ. Tessa leaped at the chance to share how God had changed her. She'd grown up in a broken home, and in her late teen years she found herself entangled in a world filled with illegal sex and substances. Only by God's grace was she not trafficked or irrevocably harmed. When Tessa finished sharing her story, the group celebrated what God had done, and everyone went back to work.

The next day a staff supervisor asked to hear the story she'd shared with her coworkers the day before. Again Tessa told about all God had brought her out of, but this time it wasn't celebrated. The supervisor said she was disappointed Tessa hadn't shared that story in the interview process. She was concerned her past would affect her ability to lead in the present and represent the church well.

Clearly, Tessa was confused. She explained that those events had occurred years earlier, before she came to Christ, and that she'd even completed therapy to find healing. But although she did her best to explain, it wasn't enough. The next day she was terminated. Not only did she lose her dream job, but she was left with the devastating feeling of being judged.

According to the book *Church Refugees*, the top reason people leave the church is "they wanted community . . . and got judgment."[1] My guess is that's not surprising to you, because you've heard of church members jumping to conclusions or fixing blame incorrectly. You may have even personally endured someone questioning your motives or commitment without knowing your situation.

Without question, the church has a giant problem with judgmentalism. But it's also a complex problem because, as believers, we're called to be examples of both God's standard and His love.

If you've been wounded by judgmentalism in some way like Tessa was, hang on. I have good news for you. But first, let's explore how judgmentalism can play out in the church—particularly between those who claim to be uncompromising and those who claim to offer unconditional love.

Condoners and Condemners Explained

Often, Christians today fall into one of two camps: they're either a *condoner* or a *condemner*. Condoners are people who live by the sentiment "It doesn't matter how you live or what you do because God is love. If you don't judge me, I won't judge you." On the other end of the spectrum, we have condemners, and their unspoken rule for living is basically "It matters a great deal how people live because God is holy. And if I see something that falls below that standard in your life, it's only right that I bring it to your attention."

What's interesting is that churches usually have a mixture of these two groups. And if they were polled, the condoners would say the condemners are mean and petty, while the condemners would say the condoners are weak and compromising. And pastors like me have the "pleasure" of playing referee between these groups.

Regardless of which way you lean, the important question is which group best represents Jesus. Is He the gentle, merciful Savior always wearing a compassionate gaze? Or is He the holy King with fiery eyes, swinging the sword of truth? The answer is yes! Jesus is both, and until we grasp how that's possible, we'll struggle to influence culture and embody Christ to the world.

One of the best examples of Jesus' being loving yet uncompromising is found in John 8. He had just entered the temple to teach when a group of religious leaders interrupted Him:

> The teachers of the law and the Pharisees brought in a woman caught in adultery. They made her stand before the group and said to Jesus, 'Teacher, this woman was caught in the act of adultery. In the Law Moses commanded us to stone such women. Now what do you say?'"
>
> John 8:3–5

You can imagine the tension this moment created. No doubt the crowd contained both condoners and condemners, and they both wanted to know where Jesus stood. Can't you just hear the condoners saying, "Leave that lady alone. She can live her life as she pleases. She can't help who she falls in love with, and she deserves to be happy"?

While that sounds compassionate and caring, it's not scriptural. To let her live a life that runs contrary to God's Word would be to let her endure the consequences of sin. As much as I appreciate a condoner's compassion, sin steals, kills, and destroys. To be silent about sin isn't compassionate; it's cruel. There's no life, no joy, and no peace in sin. Adultery destroys both homes and hearts, and to let this woman believe otherwise would not have been loving; it would have been aiding and abetting in the destruction of her destiny.

I can also imagine the condemners saying, "She should have known better. Serves her right. Her family has a history of marital issues. If she'd spent more time in the temple, this wouldn't have happened."

The thing about condemners is that they sound like they care about God's standards, but the truth is they're often just propping up their own self-worth. When I judge you, it makes me feel better about me. Spotlighting your shortcomings makes me feel superior. But because most condemners fail to realize judging others makes us slaves, that feeling is a false sense of comfort.

Researchers have discovered that judging others is a way to mask pain or shame, and it's just as common as using alcohol, food, or narcotics. It's also just as addictive. This tells us that some condemners want to stop but can't. Instead, they're stuck in "the judgment cycle," where their insecurity causes them to judge others, but then they feel shame about judging others and develop a deeper sense of insecurity.

The Problem with Judgmentalism

When we judge others, it causes God to audit us. Jesus makes this clear in Matthew 7:1–2: "Do not judge others, so that God will not judge you, for God will judge you in the same way you judge others, and he will apply to you the same rules you apply to others" (GNT).

This Scripture was fulfilled exactly as promised that day the condemners stood ready to stone this woman caught in the act of adultery (and, yes, apparently the man involved wasn't condemned, but we'll have to address double standards another time). After the scribes and Pharisees brought her to Jesus, the Bible says He knelt and began writing in the dirt. And then, "When they kept on questioning him, he straightened up and said to them, 'Let any one of you who is without sin be the first to throw a stone at her.' Again he stooped down and wrote on the ground" (John 8:7–8).

We don't know exactly what Jesus wrote, but I believe He was probably writing out each condemner's hidden sin. Maybe He wrote the names of numerous women these religious leaders had been with. Or maybe He wrote the names of those who'd cheated on their taxes or were spreading gossip and rumors. But whatever Jesus wrote displayed this truth: every time you execute judgment on others, God examines you.

As Jesus continued to write, the Bible says that from oldest to youngest, the accusers dropped their stones and left. The only one remaining was the one without sin, but He had no stone in His hand. Jesus then said, "'Woman, where are those accusers of yours? Has no one condemned you?' She said, 'No one, Lord.' And Jesus said to her, 'Neither do I condemn you; go and sin no more'" (John 8:10–11 NKJV).

Notice Jesus didn't attack her or reject her, but He also didn't say her behavior was OK. In other words, He didn't condemn or condone her. Instead, He was the perfect example of how to both hold God's standard of truth and extend His compassion to help people.

The Need for Compassion without Compromise

The apostle John makes an amazing observation in chapter 1 of his Gospel: "The law was given through Moses, but grace and truth came through Jesus Christ" (John 1:17 NKJV). Essentially, John's saying God's rules and regulations for living came through Moses, but Jesus brought us God's guidelines and coupled them with His love and power to live them out. Unlike Moses, Jesus was—and is—God in the flesh, and He's 100 percent truth and grace. Both virtues are needed to live like Jesus.

- *Without truth, there's no healing.* God's Word is the only solution for the sickness of sin, and without it, people can't change. You can give out all the compassion in the world, but if it's not coupled with the truth, all you have is a placebo. The powerful prescription that produces healing is the truth of Scripture. When you leave out the Word of God, you leave out the power of God. The Bible isn't a rulebook given by a controlling God; it's a guidebook given by a compassionate Father who desires the best for your life.

- *Without grace, no one accepts the truth.* Remember the *Mary Poppins* song "A Spoonful of Sugar Helps the Medicine Go Down"? Well, when it comes to spiritual matters, it takes a healthy dose of grace to help truth go down and take root in our life. If we're harsh and unkind, people will never accept what we say regardless of how true it is.

That's why connection must precede giving direction. There's nothing special or Christlike about someone posting something critical on social media or spouting off in a moment of anger. It's common and ineffective. What *is* unique and Christlike is when someone is willing to pursue another person, sit down with them, and lovingly say, "I'm concerned for you because your life isn't heading in the right direction. I know because I've been where you are. Let me help you find what you've been looking for."

My heart longs to see Christians more interested in helping others find a right relationship with God than in being right. To truly help someone requires a sacrifice of one's time and opinions along with a tenacity to keep saying, "I love you enough to earn the right to speak into your life."

In May 2017, a report out of England went around the globe. A man suffering from deep depression decided to take his life by jumping from a bridge near Golders Green, North London. After he made his way to the center, he climbed over the rails and stood on the edge. His life certainly would have ended that day, but before he could jump, a passerby grabbed hold of him. Almost immediately, others reached through the bars, employed some rope, and held the man for more than two hours until the authorities could rescue him from himself. This extraordinary act was captured on film and depicts many hands holding him to the bridge so he couldn't harm himself.[2]

If there's ever been a picture of what the church is called to do, it's this one! We need to tell people the truth—that leaping away from God's Word always leads to death. But we have to tell them from an uncomfortably close grip of grace, a loving grip that says, "I'm not letting you go no matter how long it takes and no matter how much you push away. I'm going to hold on to you until God gets a hold of you!"

Good News If You've Been Wounded by Judgmentalism

The woman caught in the act of adultery and brought to Jesus was healed by truth and grace. Maybe you didn't receive these two vital ingredients, and so you've lived a long time with the pain of being judged. If that's the case and you want to begin anew with Jesus, you can. And it starts with a heartfelt revelation of just how valuable you are to God.

In God's eyes, you're priceless!

Being judged hurts so much because it feels like our value is being attacked. But there's no way to ensure every person values us for who we really are. Therefore, the first step to healing comes from *decreasing* the opinion of others and *increasing* the opinion of God. What He says about you is true, pure, and life-giving, and His perspective never changes.

Now, I'll admit that one of the hardest things to communicate to people is how much they matter to God. Not because God doesn't make it clear, but because we tend to hear things like "God loves you" and quickly dismiss it. That said, let me approach this in such a way that you can truly grasp how valuable you are to Him.

First, let me say that you can tell how much someone values something by how much time they choose to invest in it. For instance, I love my wife, so she gets most of my time. But where has God chosen to spend His time? Throughout history, only the most priceless places have been graced with the presence of His Spirit.

Consider these first two places:

1. *The ark of the covenant.* This was a specially designed chest
   the Israelites fashioned, where God's Spirit would come and
   meet His people. The ark was ornate and contained some of
   Israel's most valuable possessions, like the Ten Command-
   ments. We can't fully grasp what it's worth, but the gold
   alone is valued at $63,000,000, which doesn't include the
   bronze, silver, and other precious stones. This one-of-a-kind
   container is worth millions, but God spent only a *few moments* there.[3]

2. *Solomon's temple.* After years of meeting with His people in
   the portable tent known as the tabernacle, God instructed
   King Solomon to build a temple, a house for Him to spend
   time with His people. Construction took seven years, and
   upon its completion, rulers from around the world came to
   see its beauty. The value of the gold alone would have been
   an astonishing $194,000,000,000. When we add the value
   of the silver—$22,000,000,000—Solomon's temple was
   worth $216,000,000,000. Still, God's Spirit could be en-
   gaged there only once a year.[4]

Now consider the third:

3. *You.* God has chosen to spend His time in you! First Corinthians 6:19 says, "Do you not know that your body is a
   temple of the Holy Spirit who is within you, whom you have
   received as a gift from God?" (AMP). This truth is so important that God repeats it virtually word for word in 1 Corinthians 3:16 and 2 Corinthians 6:16. And the Amplified Bible,
   Classic Edition translation for the former says, "God's Spirit
   has His permanent dwelling in you."

Think about it. For God, a multimillion-dollar box was worth only an occasional visit, and a multibillion-dollar temple was worth only an annual appearance. But *you*—despite all your hang ups and missteps—are so valuable to Him that God decided to live in you permanently.

So if God has chosen to live in you, why do you care what people think of you? Their criticism can never negate or change your worth! Knowing this in your heart will bring great healing from the judgmentalism of others.

You can treat others as the priceless treasure they are.

Once you begin catching a glimpse of how priceless you are in God's eyes, you can start showing and sharing that same loving grace you've received and they need with others.

Now, everyone responds differently to being hurt. A common response is to have an imaginary confrontation with the one who hurt you. You know, where you daydream about letting that person have it and saying all the things you wish you'd said.

I'll be the first to admit that I've rehearsed many conversations with my wounders. My words became like honed knives, and in my mind, I sliced and diced the person who did me wrong. The irony of these exercises is that they only serve to shred my inner peace and make me exactly like the person who caused me pain.

So if you've been wounded by harsh, judgmental people, you have a choice: to be like them or show them grace. The biggest part of showing grace is asking God to help you understand the life circumstances they've experienced that caused them to hurt you, and then instead of hurting them back, showing them the love of God and praying for them. Again, this is not a natural response; it's a *supernatural* response.

Everything we do is motivated by something, and when people are hurting others, it's because they're hurting.

Years ago I came across a prayer by an unknown author that's helped me change my perspective—to instead give grace. You can find more than one version of it, but this one makes my point:

Heavenly Father,

Help us remember that the jerk who cut us off in traffic last night is a single mother who worked nine hours that day and is rushing home to cook dinner, help with homework, do the laundry and spend a few precious moments with her children.

Help us to remember that the pierced, tattooed, disinterested young man who can't make change correctly is a worried 19-year-old college student, balancing his apprehension over final exams with his fear of not getting his student loans for next semester.

Remind us, Lord, that the scary looking bum, begging for money in the same spot every day (who really ought to get a job!) is a slave to addictions that we can only imagine in our worst nightmares.

Help us to remember that the old couple walking annoyingly slow through the store aisles and blocking our shopping progress are savoring this moment, knowing that, based on the biopsy report she got back last week, this will be the last year that they go shopping together.

Heavenly Father, remind us each day that, of all the gifts you give us, the greatest gift is love. It is not enough to share that love with those we hold dear. Open our hearts not to just those who are close to us, but to all humanity. Let us be slow to judge and quick to forgive, show patience, empathy and love.[5]

If you've endured the pain of being judged, you have an incredible opportunity. Instead of becoming jaded and disengaging from everyone, you can stop the problem from perpetuating by becoming an agent of grace.

You see, grace is one thing the church has to offer that the world can't get anywhere else. After all, you don't have to be a Christian to build homes for the homeless, feed the poor, or donate to charity. You also don't have to be a Christian to effect political change. Other, wise teachers offer moral instruction. But where else can the world go to find grace?

In this world, you get what you pay for. You reap what you sow. Quid pro quo. That's what makes the response of grace so powerful. There's nothing like it. When was the last time you walked through a busy store and saw grace? It rarely happens.

God is looking for people willing to show grace and stand for truth by creating a community that says, "You are welcome here! If you're addicted to something, join us. If you have some kind of sexual struggle, join us. If you lose your temper, join us. If you don't know what you fully believe, join us. You are welcome because God graciously *accepted* us, generously *loved* us, and supernaturally *transformed* us! And He can do the same for you. No judgment here—just Jesus, the embodiment of truth and grace."

Heavenly Father, though people jump to conclusions, I'm so grateful You see things as they really are. Today, I welcome Your truth and grace in my heart—truth for the places I'm out of sync with You and grace to heal from unwarranted criticisms from the past. Amen.

6

Rejection

There's a saying I've tested, tried, and proven to be true: "Ignorance is bliss." This means sometimes it's better not to know everything about a situation beforehand, because if we'd known what we would encounter on the road ahead, we would have avoided the journey.

For example, had I known how many arguments Kayla and I would have over the toilet paper roll's direction, I might not have proposed to her. Had I known how much poop a ten-pound infant can produce, I might not have become a dad. Had I known how passionate people are about the decibel level of a church sound system, I might not have become a pastor. Indeed, had I known how much a part of life is pain, I might have chosen to lock myself away.

One of the unavoidable facts of life is that it hurts. Sure, we stub toes, break bones, and have the occasional need for Icy Hot. But that's not the pain I'm referring to. The pain I'm talking about in this chapter is much deeper and lingers much longer. It's an inner pain we all encounter called *rejection*.

Respected psychologist and author Dr. Guy Winch has committed a great deal of study to the subject of rejection. He says, "Rejections are the most common emotional wound we sustain in daily life."[1]

The fact is there's not a person who hasn't been wounded by rejection. For some, it happened as a child when a teacher, coach, or parent harshly expressed their disappointment. Others experienced rejection through the act of a brutal breakup in a romantic relationship. For many, rejection happens day after day at a job they can never seem to do enough for, and yet they can't leave it because they need the income. And sadly, many people have experienced rejection in the church—the place that's supposed to offer love and acceptance.

So the question isn't whether you've been rejected. It's whether you've properly laid rejection to rest or are still haunted by the hurt.

The Pain of Rejection Can Haunt Us for Years

Summer is my favorite season. I love the longer daylight hours, the warm weather, and the endless choice of activities. I also love going to the movies to watch the latest summer blockbuster. I like few things better than sitting back with a tub of popcorn and enjoying Hollywood's latest creation—unless it's scary!

I have a great appreciation for films from just about any genre, but I've never enjoyed scary movies. I don't even like Casper the Friendly Ghost! I guess there's just something in me that believes what's passed should remain in the past.

As much as I wish that were true concerning our rejections, it's not. Even though the "event" of rejection happened years ago, it's common for the pain of rejection to still haunt us in the present.

An eye-opening example of this is found in the life of Saul, Israel's first king. Saul was chosen by God through the prophet Samuel, and for years the two men worked hand in hand to lead the nation. Over time, Saul began to stray from God's ways, causing a rift between him and his mentor.

A major breaking point in their relationship is seen in 1 Samuel 15, when Saul overtly disobeys God's instructions concerning a military campaign. When Samuel hears the news, he's enraged. He publicly humiliates Saul, severs their relationship, and rejects him as king. Though Samuel was a spiritual giant, his words deeply wounded Saul.

Three Subtle Symptoms of Rejection

Time passed, and so did Samuel, but Saul's pain remained. Insecurity and inconsistency became his constant companions—not to mention the fact that he was inconsolable. As we take a closer look at these subtle symptoms, see if they're affecting you as well.

1. *Insecure*—The *seed* of rejection always produces the *fruit* of insecurity. Saul was one of the most insecure leaders in Scripture. You can see it in his overcompensation and self-hatred. At times he was strutting in arrogance and putting down others, and at other times he was locked away mourning his mistakes. Insecurity put him in a place where he was never happy with himself or others.

   Maybe you feel similarly. You're concerned about what others think about you every time you share a thought. Every photo you post has to be perfect to cover any flaws. And every time you look in a mirror, you're reminded of what you don't like or what is (or you think is) missing.

2. *Inconsistent*—Saul's life swung like a pendulum. One minute his faith was strong and his steps obedient, and the next minute he was on the opposite end of the spectrum, swallowed up by fear and compromise. People never knew which Saul they were getting, and this ensured he never experienced momentum in any area of his life.

   If your wounds from rejection remain untreated, you may also be struggling with inconsistency. Some days you're happy, and some days you're depressed. Some days you want to change the world, and some days you want to leave the world. Some days you're passionate for God, and some days you doubt He even knows who you are.

3. *Inconsolable*—The saddest reality of Saul's life is that he never enjoyed peace, but it wasn't for lack of trying. He tried everything from substances to seances, from fame to family, from listening to David play his harp to hunting him down like an animal. Regardless of what he did, nothing could settle his soul.

Like Saul, many people whose issue of rejection has never been resolved live longing for peace. They've tried finding it through endless scrolling on social media, binging on the best that entertainment has to offer, jumping from one relationship to another, accomplishing goals, and even numbing the pain through prescriptions or other substances. But nothing has worked.

Are you one of those people?

The Danger of Digging Up the Past

Eventually, Saul's wound and the stress of an impending battle against the Philistines caused him to act in desperation. We pick up the story in 1 Samuel 28:5–14:

> When Saul saw the Philistine army, he was afraid; terror filled his heart. He inquired of the LORD, but the LORD did not answer him by dreams or Urim or prophets. Saul then said to his attendants, "Find me a woman who is a medium, so I may go and inquire of her."
>
> "There is one in Endor," they said.
>
> So Saul disguised himself, putting on other clothes, and at night he and two men went to the woman. "Consult a spirit for me," he said, "and bring up for me the one I name."
>
> But the woman said to him, "Surely you know what Saul has done. He has cut off the mediums and spiritists from the land. Why have you set a trap for my life to bring about my death?"

Saul swore to her by the LORD, "As surely as the LORD lives, you will not be punished for this."

Then the woman asked, "Whom shall I bring up for you?"

"Bring up Samuel," he said.

When the woman saw Samuel, she cried out at the top of her voice and said to Saul, "Why have you deceived me? You are Saul!"

The king said to her, "Don't be afraid. What do you see?"

The woman said, "I see a ghostly figure coming up out of the earth."

"What does he look like?" he asked.

"An old man wearing a robe is coming up," she said.

Then Saul knew it was Samuel.

Some Scriptures are encouraging, some are challenging, and some are just plain *weird*. This may be one of the weirdest. And it illustrates just how far we will go when we are haunted by hurt. Saul's soul was in so much pain that it clouded his judgment and caused him to search for relief by literally digging up the past. He revisited the one who'd rejected him, hoping to find something that would bring healing.

We do the same thing when we go through old text messages and emails, dissecting every word. As we comb through those conversations, we wonder what we could have done differently. Somehow, we hope to find something we missed or misunderstood. Like Saul, we dig and dig, failing to realize that holding on to the pain of the past damages who we are in the present.

When Saul went to consult the medium, he wore a disguise. This means he had to take off his crown and royal robe and put on the clothes of a commoner (1 Samuel 28:8). And when we dig up past pain, our true identity is undone. It's impossible to rule as royalty and be subject to the opinions of others at the same time.

According to 1 Peter 2:9, you are a royal priesthood. But when you dig up and visit past pain, you discard the royal robes God has put on you. You can't believe you're the righteousness of God in Christ Jesus and cling to rejection simultaneously. Likewise, you can't walk in your God-given authority and hold on to insecurity. For you to truly be a child of the King, you have to throw off self-rejection and the crippling opinions of others once and for all.

What's interesting about this situation recorded in 1 Samuel 28 is that many scholars believe the apparition that appeared to Saul was not Samuel's spirit but an evil spirit masquerading as the old prophet. So what appeared to be real and helpful was actually fake and hurtful to Saul. When you dig up the pain of the past, you find the deceptive voice of your spiritual enemy. And as we've learned, wounded souls are an open door for him to influence.

You can't believe you're the righteousness of God in Christ Jesus and cling to rejection simultaneously.

Saul had hoped to find peace from Samuel's rejection, but instead, the evil spirit appearing as Samuel prophesied his demise:

> All this has come upon you because you did not obey the Lord's instructions when he was so angry with Amalek. What's more, the entire Israeli army will be routed and destroyed by the Philistines tomorrow, and you and your sons will be here with me.
>
> 1 Samuel 28:18–19 TLB

The next day Saul lost his life on the battlefield just as the enemy predicted. When it comes to your situation, it's likely rejection won't result in your dying, but it can certainly stop you from living.

Reeling from Rejection

I became a lead pastor when I was still in my twenties, and I'm convinced the enemy's plan in my first two years was to wound me so deeply with rejection that I'd quit or develop a hard heart so that I couldn't fulfill my duties. And his plan almost worked!

It all started when I got an email from a leader asking for a meeting. Since this was someone I cared about and had worked with closely, I quickly set up a time. But as soon as we sat down, he informed me his family planned to vacate their leadership positions, leave the church, and find another place to worship. His explanation was that although I was a nice guy, I wasn't meeting their needs. They needed someone more like (and he named a well-known minister with a national platform).

Initially, I was shocked because I thought this was someone who supported me. Then I was angry because I'd given him a great deal of individual attention. But mostly I was broken because this seemed to be confirmation of what I was already thinking about myself—that I didn't have what it took to lead.

Over the next several months, a strange occurrence took place. Although this family had left, they seemed to always be present in my mind. I could hear their voices while I preached. It was as if they were sitting beside me every week, distracting me from what God had called me to do. That event held me hostage and robbed me of enjoying what God was doing in our church.

As I was praying one day, my mind drifted back to that conversation and I began rehashing every word. Then I suddenly heard the Holy Spirit speak loudly to my heart, *Son, until you let this die, it won't let you live.* Those words were a message of mercy from my loving heavenly Father. He was trying to wake me up to the reality that rejection was ruling my life. In that moment, something shifted in me, and I moved from digging up my past pain to the process of laying it to rest.

My prayer is that this chapter is *your* moment of mercy. That it will wake you up to the areas of your life where you're haunted by hurt and ruled by rejection, and that it will move you through the process of laying your own pain to rest. If that seems impossible, remember that all things are possible with God. Today is the day to stop digging and start burying the past!

The Road of Recovery

From that moment when the Holy Spirit spoke to me, He took me on a journey and taught me how He heals inner pain. The wisdom I've learned is what I want to share with you throughout the remainder of this chapter. It will help you recover from the pain of rejection, yes, but it can be applied to any wound from your past as well. So even if rejection isn't the wound you primarily suffer from, you can take these steps toward healing.

First, enter God's presence.

When our souls are hurting, culture says, "Sex can heal. Success can heal. If those don't work, try binge watching or binge drinking." Now, maybe you've tried one or more of these remedies, but you still haven't escaped the pain. That's because there's only one place a soul can be healed—in the presence of the One who created it.

For your soul to be made whole, it needs to be with God. Whether or not you realize it, your soul came to life with the breath of God, and you need the breath of His Spirit to sustain you. You can accomplish great feats, meet amazing people, and acquire material possessions, but your soul won't be satisfied. It was made *by* God, *for* God, and *to need* God. As author C. S. Lewis so eloquently stated, "God designed the human machine to run on Himself. He Himself is the fuel our spirits were designed to burn, or the food our spirits were designed to feed on. There is no other."[2]

When we enter God's presence, we're with the one who has everything we need. Joy is found in His presence, and heaviness is lifted. His presence can do what no pill, person, or accomplishment can. Saul ended up dead instead of delivered because he went to the enemy's presence instead of God's.

Additionally, in God's presence we're with the one who knows *what we need*. Only God can access your soul. He alone can untangle your complicated thoughts, extinguish your anger, and ignite a passion for Him where apathy has reigned. That's why David wrote,

"The Lord is my strength and my shield; in him my heart trusts, and I am helped; my heart exults, and with my song I give thanks to him" (Psalm 28:7 ESV). A rejected heart doesn't trust, and a mistrusting heart remains closed. Only God's presence can open closed hearts.

Now, allow me to dissect a significant but subtle nuance concerning the idea of God's presence. Theologically speaking, God is omnipresent, which means He's everywhere at all times. But just because He's ever-present doesn't mean we've entered His presence. We enter God's presence when we create space to worship Him and invite Him to work in us. I know a rejected heart doesn't feel like expressing worship, but worship is essential. Without God's presence our hearts never soften and open.

I recently learned what to do if you want to grow beautiful plants but have hardened soil that's difficult to till. First, saturate the area with about a half inch of water. Don't drown it; just let it soak in over time, and eventually the soil will become more cooperative and pliable. A good landscaper knows this softening process isn't a one-time event but is needed in each new season.

In a spiritual sense, this is a picture of how our hardened hearts can become receptive to the healing work of God. Life has a way of beating us down and pounding us into a hardened condition. But if we soak in God's presence again and again, our soul becomes more cooperative and pliable in His hands.

Don't rush this important step. You can't heal yourself; you need the life-giving presence of God. Only He can heal you and take away the pain of the past.

Second, acknowledge the source of your pain.

We have a basket full of single socks in our house. Somehow between the washer and dryer that are four inches apart, socks get lost. I don't know how—maybe there's a portal to another dimension or someone is playing a cruel joke. Nonetheless, the basket fills up, our sock drawers empty, and the basket stays full because we can't find what matches.

So many of us live with hurt because we can't match our current anger, sadness, or insecurity to the source of our pain—rejection. Life moves so fast, memories pile on, and additional wrongs get mixed in. Eventually, we realize something in us is off, but we can't seem to put our finger on it. We then spend our days dealing with symptoms instead of getting to the source. Oftentimes, we simply stuff our negative feelings, acting as though what we've experienced is no big deal.

If you want to heal from the pain of rejection, you must acknowledge it. You're not mad and hurt for no reason; you're mad at someone and wounded about a specific thing they did. The enemy has clouded your vision with strong emotions, hoping your hurt remains hidden. Pride doesn't want you to admit you're hurt or let your offender know they affected you. But you can't deal with what you don't acknowledge.

To experience inner healing, other people are often needed. Sadly, Saul had no close relationships. He lived in isolation, which is one of the reasons he never healed. Admitting you're hurt both to God and a trusted friend doesn't mean you're weak or that you did something wrong. It means you're human, and you're exposing the wrong done.

As a pastor, one of the most exciting moments I experience is when someone approaches me and says, "I need to tell you something I've never told anyone." Excitement builds because I know grace is being released, light is coming into a dark place, and breakthrough is approaching. Once a person admits they're hurt and identifies the source, they're moving forward on the road to recovery.

Third, decide to release your pain to Christ.

Experienced parents know the different "cries" of their children. Just by the pitch they can discern if they're seriously hurt or just expressing frustration. One day I heard our daughter Ellee crying, and I immediately recognized she was in pain. After she'd fallen and sprained her wrist, she came running through the door straight to me, sobbing and holding her arm. But the moment I reached out to assess the damage, she pulled back and exclaimed, "Don't touch it!" She came to the right person, but she didn't release me to address her pain.

I think that's a picture of so many people—they come to Jesus with their pain, but when He asks them to release it to Him, they pull back.

Indeed, nothing tests our faith like trusting someone to handle the most intimate areas of our soul. It's like choosing a doctor to perform a needed surgery. We either trust them and surrender to their work, or we never lie down on the table.

The fact is I can't heal your pain, and neither can your friends. But there is Someone who can—Jesus! He was the most rejected man to ever live. The Bible says He was despised and rejected—a man of sorrows, acquainted with bitterest grief (Isaiah 53:3). Everyone turned their back on Him and looked the other way when He passed by. The Jews, the Greeks, and the Romans all rejected Him. The Pharisees and Sadducees hated Him, and all His disciples abandoned Him in His hour of greatest need. People spit on Him, punched Him, slapped Him, mocked Him, and beat Him until He was unrecognizable.

But the worst rejection Jesus felt was in the final moments before His death—when His own Father turned away from Him because of our sins.

If you're looking for someone who understands pain, it's Jesus. He experienced criticism on every level and endured false accusations everywhere He went. You might say He majored in injustice, minored in discrimination, and earned His undergrad degree in betrayal. And His graduate degree is in humiliation with a specialty in heartbreak.

In addition to His personal experiences, Jesus knows all about your rejection. He was present for every incident, heard every word, and has collected your tears. You may be able to hide your hurt from everyone else, but not from Christ's all-seeing eyes. His spiritual MRIs reveal every part of your pain, and He won't be satisfied until you're completely healed and made whole.

The best news of all is that He can do it now! There's no rejection He can't remedy and no sorrow so deep He can't resolve it. His hand is both steady and ready to heal the hurt, but the question is whether you're willing to climb onto the table and allow Him to operate.

Releasing your pain to Jesus means you no longer go to the old places or rely on the old ways for relief. Instead, you make Jesus your only option for healing.

Finally, receive God's blessing.

The only way to ensure your never return to the pain of rejection is to receive God's blessing. By grabbing hold of what God says about you in His Word—and believing it—you won't care what anyone else says about you.

Had Saul chosen to dig into his memory of what God had said to him instead of digging in a graveyard, he would have realized he didn't need Samuel's acceptance. Years earlier, God had already told him,

> The Spirit of the LORD will come powerfully upon you, and you will prophesy with them; and you will be changed into a different person. Once these signs are fulfilled, do whatever your hand finds to do, for God is with you
>
> 1 Samuel 10:6–7

Basically, God said, "Saul, I've called you to stand out. I've given you gifts, and I promise to be with you in all you do." It's tragic to consider how Saul lived his entire life looking for something he already had.

It's been said there are two ways to live the Christian life: you can live *for* God's approval or *from* God's approval. Now, you may say, "Joe, if you only knew who I am and what I've done. I've failed so many times. How could I ever receive God's blessing?" This reminds me of a story a dear friend told me about himself.

Scott was a junior on the high school baseball team, and one day they were playing in a doubleheader. The first game was a nail-biter that came down to the last person at bat. There were two outs, and Scott's team was down by one run. Scott came to the plate with two men on base. The pitcher wound up, released the first pitch, and Scott took a big swing. He connected and hit the game-winning double. As the crowd cheered, the team jumped on Scott and carried him off the field. It was one of the best moments of his life. He was the hero!

Soon the fans settled in, and the second game started. It was another close one, and strangely, Scott's team found themselves in the exact same circumstances as the first game. Even more bizarre, Scott was once again the last at bat. Everyone had confidence in him because of how the first game ended.

The pitcher took the mound and threw the first pitch. It was a strike. The second pitch was a curve ball that Scott fouled off. When the third pitch came, it was on the edge, so Scott let it pass, thinking it was a ball. But that's when he heard the umpire shout, "Strike three! You're out! That's the ball game."

When Scott's team lost, the crowd groaned, and no players ran out to greet him. Then as my friend stood there hanging his head, knowing he'd let everyone down, he suddenly heard a familiar voice.

"That's my boy!" a man shouted. "That's my boy!" Scott looked up in the bleachers and saw his dad, Robert, cheering for him. It was as though Robert had put his arms around Scott and said, "A strikeout can't change the fact that you're my son."

Today, the weight of others' rejection and your own failures may have you believing you're less than or lacking. But your heavenly Father is looking over the balcony of heaven. And in the middle of your emotional mess and the face of your failure, He's shouting, "That's My son!" or "That's My daughter!"

Make no mistake. You are not a disappointment to God. You are the apple of His eye! You're not broken; you're His beloved. You're not what others have done to you or what you've done to yourself; you're accepted, celebrated, and treasured. Regardless of the strikes against you, no rejection can change what God feels about you. So receive His blessing and let Him heal you.

Heavenly Father, the pain of rejection has caused me to search for peace in many places, but today I recognize that You alone are able to mend my heart. In this moment, I refuse the pain from the past and receive Your blessing to live accepted as Your child! In Jesus' name, amen.

7

Sexual Abuse: Acknowledging the Pain

Let me start by saying this chapter and the next deal with the especially sensitive subject of sexual abuse. If your pain comes from such an ordeal, reading these chapters could trigger a strong emotional response, making it wise to speak with a trusted counselor. If that's the case, please do so.

In addition, please understand that the term *abuse* used throughout most of these two chapters sometimes covers both childhood sexual abuse and the abuse of sexual assault experienced by those of any age.

In 1910, renowned psychiatrist Carl Jung developed a new testing method to measure mental conflict: word association.[1] Today, this exercise is commonly used in market research, psychological studies, and as an icebreaker for parties. The process is simple:

You give a participant a word and then ask them to respond with the first word that comes to mind. For example, suppose the word given is *tree*. It would be common for the respondent to say, "Apple." Or if the word given was *beach*, it would be common for the participant to say, "Sandcastle."

Now that you understand the concept, imagine that you're the participant and the word you're given is *sex*. You might give one of many responses both common and interesting, but my guess is the last response you'd give is "Church." In most people's minds, the words *sex* and *church* could not be more disassociated. Yet Scripture has a lot to say about sex.

Contrary to what many think, sex is not a subject God avoids; He authored it. The creation account reveals that God crafted Adam and then Eve, and then He invented sex as a gift to them and blessed it. Genesis 2:25 says, "Adam and his wife were both naked, and they felt no shame." This means that within God's design, sex has no negative issues—only blessing!

I think we can all agree that humanity has drifted pretty far from sex without negative effects. Today, our world suffers from a litany of sexual problems. For instance, sexually transmitted diseases are mutating and spreading at a rapid pace. Likewise, nearly every day we hear reports of devastating sexual abuse and assault. The latest estimates show nearly 27.6 million people in the world are victims to human trafficking, with the highest percentage held for sexual exploitation.[2]

When we fine-tune our view from a global scale down to an individual scale, we must acknowledge that every person reading this book has, with little doubt, experienced some negative consequence from a relationship, act, or situation that's left them with a measure of sexual brokenness.

In light of this reality, we're all asking why things have gone so wrong. The answer to this question is complex and encompasses hundreds of factors. But if I were to give two broad reasons why we've endured so much pain, they would be that our sexuality has been undersold and that we're unaware that our sexuality is a prime target of our spiritual enemy.

The Significance of Our Sexuality Is Undersold

From Genesis and throughout the New Testament, God's design for sex is clear. Sex is to be shared by one husband and one wife who are physically, emotionally, and spiritually committed to each other for life. Anything outside of this design is outside of God's boundaries and therefore outside of His blessing. This doesn't mean God doesn't love us if we venture from His design. It just means we're outside of His best for our lives.

God defined these boundaries because it best protects the intricacy of how He created us. You and I were made as multidimensional beings with a spirit, soul, and body. Sex is an act that uniquely engages all three of these dimensions. This is where our culture undersells the significance of sex. It claims sex is *just physical*, but if that's true, then why do husbands and wives feel so betrayed when their spouse commits adultery? Why does a sexual assault carry increased trauma compared to being carjacked? And why do so many people's greatest regrets often involve something sexual?

The fact is sex is a physical act that reaches beyond your physical body. First Corinthians 6:16 explains it a bit further: "Do you not know that he who unites himself with a prostitute is one with her in body? For it is said, 'The two will become one flesh.'"

Interestingly, this passage in *The Message* paraphrase of the Bible says it like this:

> There's more to sex than mere skin on skin. Sex is as much spiritual mystery as physical fact. As written in Scripture, "The two become one." Since we want to become spiritually one with the Master, we must not pursue the kind of sex that avoids commitment and intimacy, leaving us more lonely than ever—the kind of sex that can never "become one."

The Greek word translated here as *unites* carries the idea of "bonding." This reveals that sex was designed as an adhesive to bind a husband and wife together. Regrettably, outside of God's design, sex often binds us to pain and a past we'd prefer to forget. That's why, despite our best efforts, sexual sin leads to a struggle to shake memories and emotions from people or events from long ago.

Our Sexuality Is a Major Target of Our Enemy

Satan recognizes that your sexuality is at the core of how God created you. Therefore, he's determined that if he can wound you sexually, he will have wounded every dimension of who you are and thus disable who God created you to be.

Although the enemy's intent is that we all become damaged sexually, he uses different strategies to ensnare us and inflict pain. For many, Satan's strategy is tempting us to choose to leave God's design. This is when we believe his lies, ignore God's boundaries, and embrace our own out-of-control sensual appetites. Whether it's a casual hookup, an affair, or the regular use of pornography, we've stepped out of God's design by our own choice.

Your pain, then, might not seem to quite fit the term *abuse*, but that doesn't mean it can simply be forgotten. We'll talk more about this kind of pain—and the shame it can bring—in the next chapter.

For so many the damage they experience is not of their own choosing. They're the victim of someone else's sinful choices. And without question, no subject is more heartbreaking or difficult to approach than sexual abuse. Therefore, I have to ensure we're on the same page about its definition.

The term *sexual abuse* is generally used for victims of childhood sexual trauma. Dr. Dan B. Allender says sexual abuse is defined as "any contact or interaction (visual, verbal, or psychological) between a child/adolescent and an adult when the child/adolescent is being used for the sexual stimulation of the perpetrator or any other person."[3]

You may be shocked to learn how many people this suffering encompasses. According to RAINN (Rape, Abuse & Incest National Network), the nation's largest anti-sexual violence organization, every nine minutes Child Protective Services substantiates or finds evidence for a claim of child sexual abuse.[4] Let that sink in. Before you finish this chapter, another child will become a victim.

God, protect them!

Nothing New

Sexual abuse and sexual assault aren't just modern-day problems; humanity has dealt with them for thousands of years. And sexual assault has been so widespread that God gave His people several laws concerning it—including this one recorded in Deuteronomy 22:25–27 (ESV):

> If in the open country a man meets a young woman who is betrothed, and the man seizes her and lies with her, then only the man who lay with her shall die. But you shall do nothing to the young woman; she has committed no offense punishable by death. For this case is like that of a man attacking and murdering his neighbor, because he met her in the open country, and though the betrothed young woman cried for help there was no one to rescue her.

In this passage, the word *seizes* is translated from the Hebrew verb *chazaq*, which in this form implies the violent overpowering of another person. By definition, this is not consensual, because a perpetrator has overpowered the victim. Additionally, the phrase *young woman* doesn't give a specific age, but it does imply a youthfulness that is victim to a power dynamic. At that time in history, it's likely this law mainly applied to those under the age of eighteen.

While no one should take it upon themselves to murder an accused sexual offender, this passage illustrates the sad reality of sexual abuse within society and demonstrates God's desire for victims to receive justice and be cared for.

Like God's heart, ours should break for those who have endured sexual abuse, because the effects can be long-lasting and life-shaping.

One study revealed victims of such abuse are more likely than non-victims to experience the following mental health challenges:

- They're about four times more likely to abuse drugs.
- They're about four times more likely to experience PTSD as adults.
- They're about three times more likely to experience a major depressive episode as adults.[5]

Abuse victims endure so many prolonged problems mentally, emotionally, relationally, and spiritually because the road to recovery is filled with unique challenges. They include:

A *temptation to ignore what happened.* Many victims believe it's easier to deny the past, avoid the memories, and never speak of the pain related to the abuse.

A *misunderstanding concerning what happened.* It's common for victims of sexual abuse to not recognize they're victims due to mislabeling what happened or minimizing its damage.

An *internal conflict about what they feel.* Consider the damage done to someone's psyche when abuse is intertwined with their legitimate appetite for healthy sex. The result is curiosity, confusion, and a plague of ambivalence or feeling two contradictory emotions at the same moment.

Reasons like these cause many victims to settle for numbing the pain instead of healing it. Yet in his book *The Wounded Heart*, Dr. Allender describes why feeling pain is important:

Pain is a gift. We may not welcome it when it intrudes in our life but imagine what would occur if we never felt pain. Dr Paul Brand, a renowned physician who studied and treated leprosy for many years, found that the disease destroyed its victims by numbing their nerve endings. The progressive deadening of the nerve sensations permitted the leper to put his hand or foot into dangerous situations of extreme heat, cold, or harm without awareness. The disease indirectly destroys a person by deadening his awareness of pain. The obvious parallel to our spiritual condition and life is a marvelous metaphor that brings perspective.[6]

His point is that sexually abused people often forfeit their ability to feel pain and instead focus their energy on remaining numb. But like a leper, they can eventually place themselves in dangerous situations or patterns that exacerbate what they've already endured.

If You're a Victim of Sexual Abuse . . .

If you've suffered sexual abuse, I believe God wants you to know the following:

You are not forgotten. You still bear the image of God, and the proof that you're on His heart is that you're on my heart. I have prayed for you, asking God to meet you and heal you as you read these pages. It seems that reports continually surface of abuse carried out at the hands of people who held positions of authority in churches. My stomach turns at the thought of a youth leader, pastor, or priest who was called to protect but instead used their position for personal perverted pleasure. When I think about the anger, anxiety, and loneliness you must have felt, I just cry.

So as someone in a position of spiritual authority, if you've suffered sexual abuse by someone in the church, I offer you a sincere apology. I'm sorry you weren't protected. If someone advised you to keep your abuse a secret, I apologize for that as well. I'm heartbroken you had to suffer alone. I'm grieved that the people who were supposed to look the most like Jesus instead acted like Judas.

You can choose healing over numbing the pain. I understand why you think it's better to keep it all in the past, but that's not the answer. If you haven't told anyone about the abuse, immediately find someone you trust and report what happened. The moment you share your story, the person to whom you've entrusted it becomes your advocate, someone to help carry the load. (If you're the victim of childhood sexual abuse and don't have someone you trust, call or text the Childhelp National Abuse Hotline at 800-422-4453. And if you're the victim of sexual assault and don't have someone you trust, contact the National Sexual Assault Hotline at 800-656-4673.)

It's wise to seek professional help. A trauma-informed therapist can offer you coping tips and skills to help you through your healing journey. I know in some sects of the Christian community, therapy and prescriptions are taboo. People who oppose them often pitch these practices as if they're opposed to God.

But remember, one of God's characteristics is *omniscience*. This means He has *all knowledge*. So if God possesses all knowledge and He was here before anyone else, that means all knowledge came from Him. The most brilliant minds in the world are brilliant because God shared His brilliance with them. This includes everyone in the medical and mental health community as well. I believe any prescription or therapy that's working to help you heal is help from God Himself.

You must ask yourself the most crucial question. Victimization usually isn't only an event in the past. In most cases, it's an ongoing, day-to-day experience that has the potential to grind away our faith and hope for the future. With that in mind, to begin recovering, the most crucial question to ask yourself is this: *Do I believe God is a loving Father who's committed to my healing, that He can somehow use everything I've endured for a purpose, and that surrendering my life to Him is what will bring about my restoration?*

If your answer is yes, then the path of healing laid out in the Bible, though difficult at times, is possible by having a faith that acknowledges the love, wisdom, and grace of God. If on the other hand your answer is no, then the path the Bible lays out will seem unreasonable and impossible. In essence, you don't have to believe better days are ahead yet. You just have to believe God holds your days and that He's good.

Although there's no way I can address everything you've endured or answer every question you have, I do want to ensure you're aware the enemy's goal is to use this egregious occurrence as an opportunity to escort you to the prison of *shame*. I know because that's my story.

God, there are no words to convey the grief and anger I carry. So much—security, confidence, and peace—was taken from me. It's hard to comprehend that healing is possible, but I'm leaning into the fact that nothing is impossible with You. Please help me feel again and have hope for my future. Amen.

8

Sexual Abuse:
Overcoming Shame

The local church has been a central part of my family's life for as long as I can remember. Our calendar was built around the church, and our closest friendships were formed within the church. Church was such a comfortable place that it wasn't unusual for me to wander off with friends after a service while my parents spent time talking to other members.

One evening, one by one my friends departed with their families until only an older teen and I were left. I'd just entered middle school, and I was full of insecurities and desperately desired acceptance. So when this boy invited me to hang out in his car, I didn't think anything of it. Honestly, I was thrilled he was giving me any attention at all and wanted to befriend me.

Things took an unexpected turn when he pulled a *Hustler* magazine out of his bag. This was the first time I'd seen pornography, and I was instantly introduced to a world I hadn't known existed. I was stunned and anxious—and intrigued—as he turned each page.

I'm not sure how long we sat there, but I remember he acted as a guide, offering commentary for each image. Eventually, his comments turned more personal, and he peppered me with questions like "What do you think of that?" "Would you like to do that?" and "How does seeing that make you feel?"

I became disoriented. I really wanted this guy's approval, and my curiosity was piqued, yet I knew something was wrong. I don't know what his intentions were (or if he even had any), but before anything more could happen, I heard my parents call my name. He quickly hid the magazine, and we both exited the car.

As we walked toward the small gathering of adults, he said, "Don't say anything about what we did, or you and I won't be cool." And with that instruction, I was locked inside my own mind with a batch of new emotions and experiences to process.

I realize your experience may have gone further than exposure to images. What you endured may have been physical, violent, or even criminal. But despite different levels of severity, all such encounters involve pain, and comparison never resolves pain. Just as you may still be experiencing side effects from what you encountered, that incident impacted me for years to come.

The Aftermath

Seeing those sexually charged images affected me in at least three negative ways:

It established a relationship with pornography. Many people will argue that pornography is harmless, but that simply isn't true. Countless studies have highlighted its damaging effects. Porn is so dangerous because it feeds a legitimate appetite in an unhealthy way. It also degrades our view of people to mere objects and causes us to see sex as self-serving, not sacred.

Because pornography established my initial understanding of sex, I lived in confusion for years about what healthy sex was and had a distorted view of myself and others.

It isolated me from the right people. When I was told to keep what happened a secret, I took it seriously. I told no one. But that resulted in years of pain, because anytime I had questions or struggles in this area of my life, I suffered in silence. Additionally, that this happened at the direction of a fellow believer added a layer of confusion. I wondered if I was just naïve, that many people in the church had secrets like mine.

It caused me to live with an immense sense of shame. This was the most significant impact of what I saw. Shame is an often-misunderstood emotion many equate to guilt. But guilt and shame are different. Guilt is what we feel for doing something wrong, and shame is when we feel we *are* wrong. While guilt is usually tied to a specific incident, shame is tied to the totality of our identity. In the end, shame is the constant feeling of never measuring up, being permanently flawed, and feeling separated from God. That's how I felt for many years after that incident.

Shame: The Silent Killer

Shame was the first emotion Adam and Eve felt after choosing to step outside of God's design, and it changed everything about them:

Shame changed the way they related to themselves. Scripture says they shifted from being confidently uncovered to cowering in embarrassment. The moment shame entered their souls, it lowered their self-worth and caused them to second-guess how they were made.

Shame changed the way they related to each other. Before Adam and Eve disobeyed God and shame entered their lives, they were partners and shared perfect intimacy. After shame, they were divided and blamed each other for their pain.

Shame changed the way they related to God—the most devastating result. Before shame, they walked with God every morning, and their fellowship was uninhibited. After shame, they were afraid of Him and tried to hide from His presence.

Shame ruined every aspect of their lives, and they were help-less to combat its potency. The best they could do to address their brokenness was sewing together a few leaves from a tree, hoping it would give them some sense of security. But it didn't.

Maybe that's the condition in which you find yourself. Your sense of shame—even when the abuse was not your fault—is overwhelm-ing, and it's taken all your strength just to manage each day. You've become good at sewing together solutions, but the security they provide never lasts. Like fallen leaves, they blow away when painful memories blow through your mind.

The problem is that the "leaves" we choose—whether substances, success, or acquiring more stuff—address only the symptoms of shame. Like Adam and Eve, we need more than foliage; we need our heavenly Father to address the source of our shame. Genesis 3:21 says, "The Lord God clothed [or covered] Adam and his wife with garments made from skins of animals" (TLB). The only solution for their shame was to put it in God's hands and allow Him to use the sacrifice of an innocent party to cover them.

Jesus Removed All Our Shame

What was true for Adam and Eve remains true for us. And about two thousand years ago, a completely innocent man was sacrificed on our behalf. Jesus' crucifixion was not only painful but shameful. Soldiers stripped Him, beat Him, slapped Him, spat on Him, and did every humiliating thing you can do to a human body. He was hung naked or nearly so just outside Jerusalem in an area that was the crossroads of Africa, Europe, Asia, and the Middle East. This was the equivalent of hanging Him in the central terminal of the world's busiest airport.

They cursed Him, made Him the butt of their jokes, and posted a sign above His head that read *The King of the Jews* to mock His claims of being the Son of God. As He hung there, we can be sure Satan joined in and relentlessly attacked Him, whispering thoughts of shame like *You're a failure and a fake—an embarrassment to the Jewish race and Your Father.*

Amazingly, Scripture records that in the middle of that abuse and overwhelming sense of shame, Jesus displayed an incredible determination. Hebrews 12:2 (NLV) says,

> Let us keep looking to Jesus. Our faith comes from Him and He is the One Who makes it perfect. He did not give up when He had to suffer shame and die on a cross. He knew of the joy that would be His later. Now He is sitting at the right side of God.

Because His eyes were set on our healing and full restoration, Jesus refused to give in to shame or accept its message. Purchasing our freedom from sin fueled His determination to complete His work on the cross. He was willing to endure humiliation so we could live whole. By resisting shame and resurrecting from the dead, He removed shame's power to rule our lives. The cross completely and eternally defeated shame for you and me.

The cross completely and eternally defeated shame for you and me.

But just as a person who's been given a life-saving prescription must choose to open the bottle and take what's been prescribed, we, too, must receive and take in the only remedy for sin and shame—Jesus Christ.

Please realize that even though the abuse you endured was not your choice, living with shame is. Satan wants you to think you're powerless, but that isn't true. Though it may take a great deal of time and therapy to deal with all you've endured, you can choose to overthrow shame and its poisonous effects by employing the following, proven, four-step plan of action.

1. Restore God's authority over your pain.

Wounds are so powerful that they usually reset the entire structure of our lives. In the wake of something as shattering as abuse,

107

it's not uncommon for our feelings to become the lord or leader of our lives. The grief is so strong, the anger is so acidic, and the fear is so pronounced that these emotions begin to rule our every decision, attitude, and action. That's why when we have unhealed pain, we're often unteachable and irrational.

For years I heard sermons about the risk of keeping shameful secrets, yet I never took the time to have an honest conversation with someone who could help me break free of mine. I was repeatedly warned about unhealthy patterns, but I couldn't hear and receive the truth because my feelings were in control.

Without question, your feelings are a terrible lord. Like dictators, emotions refuse to bend or give up their power. And because feelings weren't created to rule, when they're in charge they exhaust every other facet of your being. The only remedy for this malady is to overthrow your feelings' tyrannical rule.

One of the privileges I have as a dad of young kids is being well acquainted with inflatable games. Some are for jumping, and some have ball pits, but my favorite is the one that lets you joust like gladiators. Two people stand on raised platforms and attempt to knock the other off with a padded lance, and you win the game by holding the high ground and knocking your opponent off their platform.

Similarly, for your healing to begin, you have to knock your feelings off the throne of your heart so Jesus can retake His proper place as Lord. Relief comes only by restoring God's authority over your life. It's no coincidence that one of Jesus' divine titles is Prince of Peace. This tells us His ability to bring peace requires His rulership.

Now, let me forewarn you that your feelings won't give up without out a fight! They'll kick and scream, trying to convince you your circumstance is outside God's understanding and He's forgotten you. Likewise, they'll attack every principle of God's Word with painful memories and emotions. But like someone on a platform with a jousting tool in hand, if you keep swatting down every false idea and entrust your pain to God, you *will* successfully overthrow your feelings.

One thing I've learned is that healing is only for the persistent! It's for those who relentlessly say, "God, You are my Healer." It's for those who regularly pray, "God, here I am again with a flood of negative memories and emotions. Help me!" No matter how many times it takes, keep telling your feelings, "You are not in control of my life. That spot is reserved for Jesus, who is true, faithful, and has my best interest in mind." Then say, "Lord, I make You the authority over my pain."

2. Reject the lies of the enemy.

I wish in the middle of my own shame, someone would have told me that behind every wound there's a whisper. Pastor Jimmy Evans says it this way: "Wherever you find rejection, abuse, disappointment, failure, sin, sickness, trauma, and suffering, you can bet that Satan is right there, waiting to capitalize on it."[1]

We see this truth clearly demonstrated in a conversation Jesus had with His disciples about His being arrested, killed, and raised back to life. When Peter heard this, he took Jesus aside and rebuked Him: "'Never, Lord!' he said. 'This shall never happen to you!'" (Matthew 16:22).

Consider the magnitude of this moment. Peter, a mere man, is chastising the miracle-working Son of God! What would cause Peter to become so emboldened as to rebuke Jesus? I believe it was the fear of abandonment. It's very likely that in such a volatile time as the Roman occupancy of Judea, Peter had lost someone he loved dearly. While we don't know the details, it's safe to assume such a strong reaction was tied to something painful in his past.

As shocking as Peter's rebuke was, Jesus' response was even more shocking. Matthew 16:23 says, "Jesus turned and said to Peter, 'Get behind me, Satan! You are a stumbling block to me; you do not have in mind the concerns of God, but merely human concerns.'" Wow! Jesus didn't address Peter; He addressed the one speaking through Peter's pain. Jesus addressed Satan, the whisper behind the wound.

What our spiritual enemy lacks in force he makes up for with cunningness. Again, wounded people are his favorite target. He's always fanning the flames of our hurt, hoping to perpetuate our pain and lead us away from godly solutions. Sometimes he sows *anger* by whispering, "Get even." Other times he suggests *escape* by whispering, "Run to a new place, another person, or a substance." And almost every time he sows *shame* by whispering, "You deserve what happened to you."

You see, the false message within the wound keeps the wound from healing. Therefore, you can't get rid of the pain unless you get rid of the message.

Scientifically speaking, your brain is a supercomputer that efficiently executes your mind's processes, one of which is memory. Like a hard drive, your brain has recorded and stored every experience your five senses have taken in—everything you've ever smelled, seen, heard, touched, and tasted. Every word people have spoken to you is all inside. The problem is your brain doesn't distinguish between what's true and what's false.

This means many people operate on data that isn't accurate. For example, maybe when you were a kid, an adult or authority figure in your life said, "You're so stupid! You'll never amount to anything." Or "What's wrong with you?" Cutting statements like these went into your mental hard drive, and now ten, twenty, or thirty years later, they're still a core belief you're operating on.

Now, what you're about to read is important, so read it slowly. You remember things because that's how God designed your brain, but just because you remember something doesn't mean it's right. You're not what someone said about you; you're what God says about you.

When inaccurate information has caused you to live out actions or attitudes of self-defeat, you're suffering from what Scripture calls a *stronghold*. The apostle Paul expounds on this in 2 Corinthians 10:3–5 (NLT):

We are human, but we don't wage war as humans do. We use God's mighty weapons, not worldly weapons, to knock down the strongholds of human reasoning and to destroy false arguments. We destroy every proud obstacle that keeps people from knowing God. We capture their rebellious thoughts and teach them to obey Christ.

The original Greek word here for *stronghold* means "to fortify," and it depicts an ancient fortress built on the highest peak of a city. This castle-like structure was made of thick, impenetrable walls, and in times of war, this stronghold is where leaders hid while they continued to direct their followers. Spiritually speaking, a stronghold is a fortified pattern of thought that directs our lives according to the enemy's plan.

The telltale sign that you're dealing with a stronghold is when you experience thinking that argues with and goes against God's Word. Any thought pattern that causes you to accept less than God's best or consistently aggravates your emotional state is a stronghold. When ungodly thinking dominates your life, you're left with only one choice: reboot your mind with God's Word!

When it comes to the mind, you can't stop a thought; you can only replace it.

Let me be clear. By rebooting, I don't mean rehearsing painful memories or trying to resist bad thoughts and emotions. Those practices don't work, and I can prove it. Think about a *red truck*. Can you see the red truck in your mind? Good! Now stop thinking of a red truck. Put every example of a red truck out of your mind. Just stop picturing that truck that's red.

Impossible, right?

Now try this. Think of a *blue car*. Can you imagine a blue car in your mind? Can you see the doors and windows of the blue car? Of course you can. And while you're thinking of the blue car, what have you stopped thinking about? That's right! The red truck. This tells us that when it comes to the mind, you can't stop a thought; you can only replace it. So when I say to reboot your mind, I mean to intentionally confront bad thoughts and replace them with God's thoughts every day:

- If your stronghold causes you to say, "I'm damaged, broken, and beyond repair," replace that lie by saying, "I am a new creation in Christ! What happened to me no longer has control of me." (2 Corinthians 5:17)
- If your stronghold causes you to say, "I'm incapable of love," replace that lie by saying, "The cross proves I am completely loved by God and therefore capable of loving others." (Romans 5:8 and 1 John 4:19)
- If your stronghold causes you to say, "I'll be tormented by what happened to me for the rest of my life," replace that lie by saying, "I will smile, sleep sweetly at night, and celebrate life, because I've been given peace and joy through the Holy Spirit." (Proverbs 3:24 and Romans 14:17)

By putting in the work to identify your stronghold and finding a Scripture to address it, spiritually speaking, you've downloaded the thoughts of God, and they will upgrade your thoughts, attitudes, and actions to free you from the lies of the enemy. This is how you turn a simple verse into a significant victory.

3. Rest in God's justice.

Shame settles so deeply in our soul because it's tethered to our resentment, and like an anchor, resentment keeps our shame from being moved. The answer to this dilemma is to rest in God's justice.

We often hold on to resentment because it's our way of punishing someone. Subconsciously, we feel as though we're taking revenge. But when we practice this, we're living in direct opposition to Scripture. Consider these instructions in Romans 12:17–19 (TLB):

Never pay back evil for evil. Do things in such a way that everyone can see you are honest clear through. Don't quarrel with anyone. Be at peace with everyone, just as much as possible. Dear friends, never avenge yourselves. Leave that to God, for he has said that he will repay those who deserve it. Don't take the law into your own hands.

I love the brilliance of Scripture, because it acknowledges that what the offender did needs to be addressed—just not by us. Why? Because revenge takes emotional energy, and God's desire is that we focus all our energy on being healed. That's why He says, "Leave the payback with Me. I'll avenge it."

When we forget that God sees all our hurts, we think we have to take matters into our own hands. But when we attempt to settle the score, we prevent God from settling the pain in us.

Think about it. Who can do a better job of avenging a wrong? You or God? If you answered God, then why are you holding on to your resentment? I suggest it's because you think if you stop remembering the hurt, the offender will get away with what they did. Thus, resentment is our way of keeping a record of what they did so it won't be forgotten.

When a crime is committed, a detective goes through a tedious process of collecting evidence and filling out a report. Then everything concerning that crime is filed away and kept under guard. These efforts are to ensure nothing is missed and justice can be served.

Did you know God has a similar process? Psalm 56:8 says He collects and stores all your tears (TLB). They're a record of what was done to you. Every time you were mistreated, abused, rejected, or experienced prejudice, God made note of it. So you don't have to keep resentment; you can rest in God's justice. Nothing has slipped by His watchful eye, and not only can He execute justice, but He can heal you. He just won't go to work as long as the resentment remains in your heart.

4. Believe better days are ahead.

Shame has a way of claiming we've reached the end of our quota of good days. It persistently conveys the idea that our best days are behind us and we're left with only bad memories and dashed dreams. But shame's claim doesn't stand up to the story of countless people who have allowed God to redeem the pain of their lives.

I've seen it with my own eyes. Several years ago, my friend Bruce Deel invited me to tour the campus of a ministry he founded called The House of Cherith. It's a trauma-informed residential recovery program that provides a safe place for female survivors of sexual abuse and exploitation. They have three locations across the state of Georgia, and the uniqueness of the program is that it addresses all the components a woman needs to relaunch into a better life— community, treatment, vocational training, housing, and family unification.

Bruce says, "When these women arrive, they're broken in every way you can be broken—physically, mentally, emotionally, spiritually, and relationally." The day I visited the campus, I heard countless stories that validated his assessment.

One resident shared how she lost her virginity at sixteen to a thirty-six-year-old man in her neighborhood. He'd coaxed her into the act by introducing her to illegal drugs, for which she quickly developed an addiction. Then her need for a fix created leverage for her abuser's aunt to pimp her out for the next year.

Another resident said, "My trauma began at age three and continued for years. My abusers included my father, maternal uncles, maternal grandfather, and every boyfriend I ever had. By my early teens, I recognized sex was the only way I could provide for myself, so I sold my body from age fourteen to twenty-six."

One resident shared how she'd had a troubled childhood. In response, her family moved to a new neighborhood, and there, as a teenager, she met a "Christian" guy who became her boyfriend. They attended church together, but over time she learned he was a member of a local gang. Under his direction, she began having sexual experiences with other gang members, then became a stripper at sixteen. At age eighteen, she was kidnapped and then trafficked for the next twelve years.

After hearing what those residents shared, it would be easy to assume the anger and shame they carried was too much to recover from. But that assumption would be far from correct. Though each story had a gut-wrenching and heartbreaking beginning, they'd also taken a beautiful turn for the better. Through treatment and God's grace, each of these women rediscovered her self-worth, obtained her GED or a technical certificate, and acquired a well-paying job. Some had regained custody of their children.

Most important, they each had vibrant relationships with Christ, and to my amazement, nearly every one of them was somehow serving others who were hurting and walking a similar road to recovery. God had taken their greatest pain and given it a purpose.

As a victim of sexual abuse, it's probably hard for you to believe, but your story hasn't ended. Instead, it's at the crucial turning point where your testimony is being shaped by God. As with these amazing women who endured tremendous hardship, God is working all things together for your good so that you—like Joseph, mistreated by his brothers—can say to those who hurt you, "Even though you planned evil against me, God planned good to come out of it. This was to keep many people alive, as he is doing now" (Genesis 50:20 GW).

God, my days of hiding in shame are over! I've come to You because I know You make all things new. Therefore, I choose to make Your Word the authority of my life—what it says is what I believe! I declare that what happened to me no longer limits what You can do through me. In Jesus' name, amen.

9

Disappointment with Leaders

If you look around you, you'll see we're a culture obsessed with leadership. Reading or watching biographies is one of the most popular forms of entertainment, and most of our 24-hour news cycles are focused on the motives and movements of those in charge. At one point Amazon offered more than sixty thousand books with the word *leadership* in the title, and according to one report, "organizations around the globe invest approximately $46 billion annually on leadership development programs."[1]

What's surprising about all this is that even though there's more information on the topic of leadership than ever before, our world has never seemed to have a greater deficit of effective leaders than it does now. A *Forbes* article said a recent study showed that only about 35 percent of employees felt inspired by their boss.[2] Less than half of US adults (44 percent) said they had a great deal or fair amount of confidence in people who held or were running for public office.[3] And only 31 percent of Americans said they had a great deal of confidence in the church or organized religion, which was a record low in Gallup's tracking poll.[4]

Are you one of the many who have lost confidence in a faith leader? C. S. Lewis said, "Of all bad men religious bad men are the worst."[5] I think he was acknowledging that the failure of a faith leader carries an extra measure of sting because the nature of their calling is to display better than others the character of the One who called them. Sadly, the reality is that many people who lead in the name of Jesus lead nothing like Jesus.

Types of Toxic Leaders

Faith leaders display many different types of toxicity, and to list them all would take a book much longer than this one. That said, I believe if we were to share our experiences, most of the people who were "less than leaders" in our lives would fall into one of five categories.

Dishonest leaders. Since trust is the foundation of every relationship, dishonesty is the quickest way to implode one. Whether it's a promise not carried out or a lie told to hide ulterior motives, when a faith leader fails to do what he or she says, our hearts are affected, and those effects carry both short-term and long-term ramifications. In the short term, we become unable to receive from them because we question everything they do. In the long term, we settle into second-guessing all leaders—even those with integrity.

Apathetic leaders. Sometimes the frustration we have with those over us isn't centered on what they do but what they don't do. We see injustice, yet they remain silent. We see opportunity, but they let it pass by. We have conversations, offer to help, and pray for them to have fresh vision, but like the Old Testament priest Eli, they settle for the status quo. Under these kinds of leaders, our passion slowly erodes and is replaced by growing criticism in our hearts. Before long, we're left with the gnawing question, *What should I do?*

Arrogant leaders. As much as I wish it wasn't so, sometimes people choose to lead for the betterment of themselves, not others. Nothing strokes the fragile egos of leaders like building entire ministries around themselves. This is especially toxic for churches, because arrogance is a cousin to entitlement, and entitlement is the father of so many sins. Arrogant leaders don't just hurt those inside the church; they also hurt those outside the church. That's because when we exchange humility for celebrity, we obstruct the flow of God's grace, making us unable to deliver the life change promised in God's Word. In essence, arrogance makes the church an empty shell instead of a channel of transforming power.

Controlling leaders. These leaders display their toxicity in many ways, including through intimidation, manipulation, and insinuation. At the core, a controlling leader is motivated by fear. These insecure individuals inflict pain on those they're leading through mind games, gaslighting, micromanagement, and by denying them the privilege of being led by the Holy Spirit. According to 2 Timothy 1:7, God never leads by fear—that's the mark of our spiritual enemy. God leads through peace (Colossians 3:15). I hate to say it, but the devil is using fear to deceptively influence the decisions of many church leaders.

Compromised leaders. These are the kind of toxic leaders we're most familiar with and are often most wounded by. They're the ones we hear about in articles, depositions, and documentaries. While they seemed to have it all together, we later learn there was more to their story. They're the ones who cause us to feel compassion for their family, carry frustration with their actions, and ask questions about their future. What usually follows the news of their embezzlement, infidelity, or addiction, for example, are countless damaging conversations we hear around the community. This results in a loss of confidence in ourselves—namely, in our ability to choose leaders.

Although each of these types of toxic leaders carries a distinct dysfunction and provokes a unique reaction, if you had to boil down the lingering feeling left in our hearts from what they did, it would be disappointment. For some of you, that word seems too soft, because a leader's ungodly actions have cost you so much. You may have lost a job or even your reputation because of what they did. But while I would never want to minimize what you endured, I believe disappointment plays a major role in the mixture of emotions you feel.

Disappointment Is Deadly

Make no mistake—disappointment isn't to be taken lightly. Yes, anger is acidic, and grief is smothering, but if disappointment is left untreated, it can detrimentally affect your faith.

To help us understand what we're dealing with, here's a basic definition: disappointment is when our *reality* doesn't meet our *expectations*.

We enter into every situation hoping it turns out a certain way. But occasionally those hopes are dashed, and that's the opportunity disappointment seizes. Every time you placed yourself under a leader, you expected them to steward your trust, and the fact that one or more of them didn't is what opened the door to disappointment.

Let me be clear. There's nothing wrong with being disappointed. It's as natural as breathing. The problem occurs when you allow it to remain in your heart, the center of your spiritual life. God designed your heart to be ruled by peace, but long-held disappointment is like an infection that slowly makes your heart sick. In your weakened state, your spiritual enemy seizes an opportunity to plant the idea that if God was trustworthy or had a good plan for your life, He would have placed a better leader over you. Thus, you think, this failure of leadership is ultimately God's failure.

The enemy's goal through disappointment is to plant enough doubt in your mind that you'll hold back portions of your heart from God. If you do that, then you're not living out one of God's foundational commands: "Trust in the LORD with all your heart and lean not on your own understanding" (Proverbs 3:5). Without your whole heart, God's work in your life is limited, and you start leaning on yourself.

The telltale sign this is happening in your life is you've stopped seeking God's counsel or sharing your true feelings with Him. Many people fall into this trap because they have an incorrect image of Him. They assume He doesn't care or only wants to hear from them when they've been good and feel good. Therefore, in seasons of frustration, grief, and disappointment, they avoid God or put on a plastic smile, calling it faith and acting like nothing's wrong. But withholding how we truly feel never leads to healing.

For this reason, you must regularly get gut-level honest with God. I encourage you to consider journaling about how frustrated you are or taking a walk and pouring out your anger. Another option is to simply sit in a quiet space and share your feelings. And if you need to, cry. I've found nothing honors God more than being open and honest with Him. When you take your pain to Him, it says, "I trust You."

Proven Practices for Gaining and Maintaining Peace

While moments of honesty and transparency with God certainly bring relief, the real work of dismantling disappointment will have just begun. You may still be under the leadership of the person who let you down or still be affected by their decisions. To maintain and grow in your newfound peace, you need to know about some proven practices, and that's what we'll focus on for the remainder of this chapter.

Rest in God's Faithfulness

Disappointment is dangerous to our souls because it slowly diminishes our expectation of what God can do. Think of it this way: disappointment is the seed that brings a crop of doubt. Each time you're let down, disappointment is planted in your heart, and if unchecked, over time it grows like a weed that chokes out your faith.

Doubt damages your destiny because it limits what God can do. The only response that effectively combats this is to reflect on how He has been faithful in the past. Lamentations 3:21–23 says, "This I recall to my mind; therefore, I have hope. The LORD's lovingkindnesses indeed never cease, for His compassions never fail. They are new every morning; great is Your faithfulness" (NASB).

Here God clearly tells us that remembering what kind and faithful things He's done in the past relieves our concern about what might happen in the future. Practicing this isn't hard. It just requires you to pause and engage in the art of reflection. I bet within seconds you could recount events of how God protected you, provided for you, made a way for your family, connected you to the right people, opened the right doors, or brought you through grief and trouble. As you recall God's kindness and faithfulness, you'll notice that remembering them generates a genuine heart of gratitude, and then faith begins to flow!

In light of all He's done in the past, isn't it fair to assume He'll be faithful to see you through your present season of trouble and transition? If He was capable of handling your problems then, don't you think you can trust Him to resolve the problems you're facing now? As you purposefully remember all the many ways God has blessed you, you'll find rest in His faithfulness.

Recalibrate Your Expectations

Humanity's capacity to accomplish great feats is quite remarkable. It's displayed in building structures like the pyramids, climbing mountains like Everest, and making jaw-dropping journeys like the ones to the moon. Yet as amazing as our accomplishments can be, we're still so far from perfection.

Isn't it funny how we know that, and yet every time someone fails us, we're surprised? This is why we must continually recalibrate our expectations of the people around us. We must remember that Jesus didn't call us to follow His followers but to follow Him.

Personally, I think it's wise to adopt God's expectations for people, and we catch a glimpse of them in Psalm 103:13–14: "The LORD is like a father to his children, tender and compassionate to those who fear him. For he knows how weak we are; he remembers we are only dust" (NLT).

Did you catch it? God expects from us what He expects from dust! No more and no less. He knows that even at our best, we're limited, flawed, and as inconsistent as the blowing of the wind. Now, let me be clear. This passage doesn't mean we should set the bar so low that the actions and attitudes of those leading us should go without accountability. It simply means we should keep in mind that leaders have limitations, and because we know that, we can predetermine to extend grace when those limitations are displayed. That's the disposition God has toward us.

The fact that the passage says the Lord is like a father reminds me of a trip to Disney World our family took a couple of years ago. In one of the exhibits, you can draw with a Disney artist. So because our kids love art, we sat in a session as a family. The artist showed us how to shape and shade the selected character, and at the end of the session, we all compared our drawings.

Sawyer, our oldest, is a natural artist, so his drawing looked terrific. I, on the other hand, have very little artistic ability, so mine looked like it was painted by a blindfolded elephant (no offense to pachyderm fans!).

When I asked to see my daughter Sydney's picture, her eyes filled with tears as she told me, "Mine is horrible. I'm a terrible artist." Again and again, she exclaimed, "I tried hard, but it's so bad!" My heart broke for my little girl. There we were in what's called the happiest place on earth, but she was miserable because of the unrealistic expectations she'd placed on herself.

Yet as I picked up her picture, I thought, *Wow! This is really good for her age.* I was impressed, because as her father, I understood her capacity.

One of the most comforting thoughts about God is that He understands our capacity. When He looks at us, He doesn't criticize or condemn. Instead, He says, "For dust, you're doing pretty good! I made you with limited wisdom, strength, and energy because I made you to need Me. I already factored your failure into the equation."

Knowing that God extends grace toward me makes it easier to extend grace to my leaders. Remember, what we receive from God we're to freely give to others—by the grace He gives us.

Recognize and Submit to God's Authority

Part of being a follower of Christ is choosing to follow God's Word despite what our feelings tell us. We are the Lord's and we're called to *submit* to His leading. Jesus gives us the ultimate example of what submission looks like. Rather than give in to His human desires to avoid the cross, He submitted to the Father, praying, "Not my will, but yours be done" (Luke 22:42).

That same calling was extended to all of Jesus' followers when Peter wrote,

> Servants, be submissive to your masters with all [proper] respect, not only to those who are good and kind, but also to those who are unreasonable. For this finds favor, if a person endures the sorrow of suffering unjustly because of an awareness of [the will of] God.

> 1 Peter 2:18–19 AMP

This is likely not the passage you've hung on your wall or chosen as a background for your phone's screen. Yet there's life-changing power when we put this instruction into practice.

To be clear, submission doesn't mean being someone's doormat or to live without protective boundaries. Likewise, submission doesn't mean giving your leader a blank check so they can force you to do unlawful or ungodly things. In the original Greek language, the word for *submission* is a military term implying a higher command has assigned and ordered all troops. For our purposes, submission is a mindset that recognizes God as the highest-ranking authority, and He's established all authority—civil, church, family, and social—to either teach us, protect us, or correct us. He orders our steps within that structure.

You may have just blurted, "Joe, there's no way God would choose the person I'm under or want me to submit to them considering how ungodly they are." But submission has nothing to do with having a superb leader. It's about obeying God's Word. Peter went on to write, "Show proper respect to everyone, love the family of believers, fear God, honor the emperor" (1 Peter 2:17). How is this even possible? I believe it's by the grace God gives us. Notice Peter said to "fear God" *before* he instructed us to "honor the emperor." You and I can always submit to lesser authorities—even bad ones—when we trust God as the ultimate authority.

A vital aspect of submission is believing and trusting that God is the one who assigned you to where you are. While many tend to think we choose the church, job, or ministry where we serve, I believe God providentially assigns each of us. First Corinthians 7:17 says, "Each person should live as a believer in whatever situation the Lord has assigned to them, just as God has called them." So just as God assigns leaders to specific places, He assigns followers for His purposes.

"Well, why would God assign us to difficult people and circumstances?" you ask. To develop us! While you may think toxic leaders are just a result of Satan's doing, you need to realize God will use them to accomplish His plan too. We see this principle play out all through Scripture. God often placed His people under terrible leaders to turn those people into great leaders. Just ask Moses about Pharaoh, David about King Saul, and even Jesus about the Pharisees. When God wants to increase our capacity, He often uses toxic leaders to do so, because adversity increases our capacity.

When God wants to increase our capacity, He often uses toxic leaders to do so, because adversity increases our capacity.

The Bible tells us that the moment you and I became followers of Jesus, God deposited His DNA inside us (1 John 3:9). This includes the divine seeds of His temperament, which we know as the fruit of the Holy Spirit.

What may surprise you is that bad leaders, broken cultures, and difficult seasons create the perfect conditions for the seeds of love, joy, peace, patience, kindness, gentleness, goodness, faithfulness, and self-control to grow. God often uses bad leadership to grow our character. The question is whether you *resist* God's process of development or *welcome* it.

God planted seeds of greatness in Joseph. But for those seeds to grow, God had to place him under brothers who abused him, a government official named Potiphar who mistreated him, and a prison warden who took advantage of him. Psalm 105:19 says, "Until the time came to fulfill his dreams, the LORD tested Joseph's character" (NLT). I'm certain Joseph wanted to resist and abandon God's testing, which may be what you're tempted to do when faced with a disappointing leader.

It's common today for people to abandon situations at the first sign of difficulty—a challenging person or circumstance. They change jobs or churches seemingly as frequently as they change underwear. But what they fail to realize is that God is in the difficulty, working on their character. Every time they quit, they also quit God's development.

If you're thinking about quitting, consider this: God doesn't promote until His purpose is fulfilled. Joseph didn't enjoy serving his brothers, organizing Potiphar's household, or administrating the prison. Nevertheless, he determined, "I will show grit rather than quit!" He could sense God was at work, and when his character was ready, he was promoted from a prison to a palace.

When your character is ready, God will release your promotion—so don't quit!

Refuse to Be Disrespectful—Honor Instead

When you're under a difficult leader, the temptation is to disrespect them. Rather than use words, we tend to do things like give less than our best, keep a mental log of all their worst moments, or make statements that undo their influence or reputation.

But God anticipated this temptation, which is why He prompted Peter to write, "Don't repay evil for evil. Don't retaliate with insults when people insult you. Instead, pay them back with a blessing. That is what God has called you to do, and he will grant you his blessing" (1 Peter 3:9 NLT).

What Peter is referring to is the concept of honor. Most people would consider themselves honoring of others, yet that can't be true because our world is growing more dishonorable every day. Somehow what we claim and what we carry out don't line up. We understand what it means to cancel or condemn, but honor is a concept we simply don't grasp.

At the core of our misunderstanding is the idea that we're to give honor based on what people deserve. We've redefined what Scripture teaches and made it about performance. But as long as honor is about performance, we'll always have a reason not to offer it. Yet the Bible clearly teaches honor isn't optional. Peter says we should "honor everyone" (1 Peter 2:17 ESV). I'm no Greek scholar, but the word *everyone* seems to exclude no one. This means honoring is decided, not necessarily deserved.

Ultimately, honor is when I treat you like God would treat you despite how you've treated me. Honor isn't based on your view of someone; it's based on God's view of them. He has a unique ability to see our depravity and our destiny at the same time. He sees beyond our past and present failures to what we will become once He's done with maturing us. By His grace, this is how we must view people if we want to be a person of honor.

Honor isn't based on your view of someone; it's based on God's view of them.

I realize how challenging this can be, but don't forget the last part of 1 Peter 3:9: "[God] will grant you his blessing" (NLT). Honor is always rewarded. I know this is true because I've lived it. I've done plenty of dishonorable things in my life, and I've noticed that when I'm dishonorable, things never go well. That's because God doesn't honor those who go around dishonoring others.

In contrast, though, God has lifted me to heights I couldn't have achieved on my own when I've chosen to compliment my leaders' strengths (despite their apparent weaknesses) and give my best (despite being underappreciated).

So when you're tempted to be disrespectful, remember that the amount of favor God pours on you will be proportional to the amount of honor you pour on others.

Realize That Sometimes the Toxicity Is in You

Early in my ministry, I served at a church navigating some restructuring. Change is always a challenge for churches, so it wasn't a surprise that staff members and volunteer leaders were struggling.

Young leaders are a gift because of their passion, but passionate leaders can also be opinionated. I assumed my opinions about how the restructuring should be handled were the only way it should be done. The problem was some of my opinions were different from the lead pastor's. When a few of the calls he made produced poor outcomes, I thought that was my license to criticize him. In my mind, I was right, the lead pastor was wrong, and the results proved it.

At first, I shared my thoughts only with my wife. But then I started sharing them with friends in ministry in other cities. Time passed, and somehow I thought my opinions were so insightful that I couldn't help but share them with some of the other staff on our team. As you may have guessed, what I was saying got back to the lead pastor.

One day he asked me to join him for lunch, and because I was unaware he knew what I'd been doing, I assumed he wanted my take on how to better our situation. But over Chinese food, he revealed that he knew about my critical comments, how they disappointed him, and that because of my actions he'd decided to remove me from the restructuring team. Although I was outwardly respectful in the moment, inside I was furious. His decisions had proven to be wrong, and what I'd suggested had proven to be the right calls.

What I didn't understand was that often the dysfunction we see in someone else blinds us to our own. I was so focused on his bad decisions that I didn't realize I was operating in pride.

If you're in a situation of disappointment with a leader, is it possible that the toxicity you see in him or her is blinding you from seeing something toxic in your own attitude or actions? I ask this because rarely in conflict is one party completely responsible and the other party completely innocent.

What I thought was poor leadership that day at lunch was actually godly correction. The idea that godly correction is a "normal" part of someone's maturity is missing in many faith communities today. It seems the first time a leader questions an action or attitude, they're vilified, perhaps assassinated online. But the apostle Paul informs us that correction is part of our calling:

> A servant of the Lord must not quarrel but must be kind to everyone, be able to teach, and be patient with difficult people. Gently instruct those who oppose the truth. Perhaps God will change those people's hearts, and they will learn the truth.
>
> 2 Timothy 2:24–25 NLT

Notice he says it's the leader's responsibility to (gently) correct, but it's the other person's responsibility to change. It took some time, but with the help of the Holy Spirit, I concluded that my actions and attitude were wrong.

If you and a leader God has placed over you are in conflict, take time to ask God what He's doing. Is He developing your character? Is He teaching you the principle of honor? Maybe He's using that person to show you something about yourself that needs to change. If so, receive the correction humbly and quickly. This will enable you to advance in what God has for you.

Though I disagreed with my leader, I'm so thankful he displayed gentleness in how he handled me. It opened my eyes, grew my character, and made me a better leader!

God, few things are harder than being disappointed by a leader. Please remind my heart that all have sinned and fall short of the glory of God. Additionally, help me overcome my disappointment by turning it into determination to forgive others' failures, to honor those over me, and to steward whatever influence You've given me. In Jesus' name, amen.

10

Wounding Words

Like most kids, I grew up playing baseball, and I'll never forget one of my first games as a Little Leaguer. Out of the gate, we played one of the best teams in the league, and my first time at bat I faced their hardest-throwing pitcher. This guy didn't seem like a Little Leaguer! In fact, I could've sworn he had a mustache and drove himself to the game.

When he threw his first pitch, it hit me square in the ribs. It took a few moments, but once my lungs refilled with air, I got up and finished the game.

That event forever changed how I played baseball. From that moment on, I focused more on protecting myself than playing to win. Everything became about not getting hurt again.

This story reminds me of how deeply hurtful words can affect us. Once someone's negative comments penetrate and wound our soul, we tend to change how we approach life. Everything becomes about not getting hurt again. That's why some people are passive and allow others to run over them—they're hoping to avoid conflict. It's also why others keep certain individuals at arm's length. Somehow they believe they won't get hurt again if those people can't get close.

If you've been hurt by the demeaning and destructive words of others, recovery is possible. The negative effects can be reversed by identifying self-defeating thoughts, reinstating God as your great-est authority, and believing what God says about you rather than what others say.

A Powerful Example of the Power of Words

Let me draw your attention to an interesting story regarding the power of words. You may have heard of a man named Abraham whom God called out of the land of Ur and to whom He promised to birth a mighty nation. It was through Abraham that Isaac was born, but it was through Jacob, Isaac's son, that Abraham's family tree really began to multiply. Jacob had twelve sons, and at the birth of his youngest the power of words was put on full display:

> Then they moved on from Bethel. While they were still some dis-tance from Ephrath, Rachel began to give birth and had great dif-ficulty. And as she was having great difficulty in childbirth, the midwife said to her, "Don't despair, for you have another son." As she breathed her last—for she was dying—she named her son Ben-Oni. But his father named him Benjamin.
>
> Genesis 35:16–18

To the casual reader, it may seem strange that Jacob would op-pose his dying wife's wish to name her son Ben-Oni. But if you take a closer look, you'll see Ben-Oni means "son of sorrow." This is the type of name that wouldn't be easily shaken but would set the course of one's entire life. Every time someone called this man's name, each time he signed an agreement, he'd relive the sorrow he caused his mom through his birth.

Now, you probably weren't given a name that means "son of sor-row," but I guarantee you've been wounded by someone's words. In fact, my guess is that the sting of those words is still lingering in your ears. You heard phrases like:

"Always a bridesmaid, never a bride."

"You don't have what it takes."

"Why can't you be more like your brother [or sister]?"

"Can't you do anything right?"

And worst of all, "I don't love you anymore."

The painful things family, friends, and coworkers say are tough enough, but what about when the poisonous speech you encounter comes from those in the household of faith? There's something extra hurtful when a fellow believer, who's supposed to build us up, tears us down. Whether it's a snarky comment from a resident "Pharisee" about something you're wearing or from a well-meaning person who's super opinionated about something in your life, the reality remains that most church hurt comes wrapped in words.

In that moment when Jacob's youngest son was being born and his dying mother pronounced that his name was to be Ben-Oni, Jacob, his father, said, "Stop! Don't write that on the birth certificate. His name will not be Ben-Oni. It will be Benjamin, meaning "son of my right hand" or "son of blessing." In that moment, the words spoken over this boy's life went from sorrow to celebrated. A wound was instantly averted, and a blessing was released because his father stepped in.

You Are What God Says You Are

The experience Benjamin had is what God wants you to have. As your heavenly Father, He desires to stop the wounding words of others and pronounce His blessing over your life. I touch on this in other chapters, but according to Him, you're not what others say you are. You're not your past mistakes nor your shortcomings. You are His child, made in His image. You are loved, adored, and celebrated.

Others may call you a burden, but your Father says you're a *blessing*. Others may call you a failure, but your Father calls you *forgiven*. Rather than your being broken, as some claim, your Father says you're perfectly formed. And His plan for your life will not be stopped by the words of others!

You should be very glad that Jacob rose to the occasion to ensure his son's name was Benjamin. Scripture records Benjamin's life was indeed blessed, and generation after generation of his descendants served God, including someone who's responsible for you and me knowing Christ today. I'm talking about the apostle Paul. According to Philippians 3:5, Paul was of the tribe of Benjamin. He wrote about two thirds of the New Testament, and his writings to the Gentiles opened the way for the entire world to hear the message of Jesus.

How important is it to be healed from wounding words? If you hold on to the hurt, God may not be able to impact everyone He wants to impact through you. Therefore, if you recognize you're living with unwanted limitations because of something hurtful said to you, it's time to deal with the record of negativity that's affecting your soul.

Now, let me warn you: wrong words take work to remedy. I wish there was a magic wand that could be waved over you to remove every painful syllable, but I've yet to discover one. The only way to remove hurtful words is through intentional, tedious effort. But don't be afraid! The Holy Spirit will lead you through the process, giving you the strength you need to know and believe what God says about you.

Undoing the Effects of Wounding Words

Here are some of the ways you can undo the effects of wounding words:

Identify Your Self-Defeating Thoughts

Make no mistake, thoughts are powerful because they ultimately produce actions. Scripture says, "As he thinks in his heart, so is he" (Proverbs 23:7 NKJV). A word becomes a thought, a thought becomes a feeling, a feeling becomes an action, actions become a habit, and habits create a lifestyle. Allowing self-defeating thoughts to remain unchecked is asking to experience a lifetime of pain.

I recently read that the average person has more than sixty thousand thoughts per day, and more than 80 percent of them are negative.[1] That means most people live in a fog of negativity that seems impossible to overcome. Negative thoughts exist for many reasons, but one of the most common is that although they sound like your thoughts, they're usually the residue of someone's words.

For example, you may hear *I'm stupid* in your mind, but that's because an unkind teacher once said, "You're not very bright, are you?" Or you may commonly think to yourself, *I'm so fat,* and that's because one time someone told you, "You'd be so much prettier if you lost weight." Or maybe you repeatedly think *I'm doomed* because someone once highlighted a series of poor choices you made.

Whatever your recurring, self-defeating thoughts are, write them down, and then begin investigating each one to determine where it originated. Get the Holy Spirit involved in your search. Although you and I can't know what's in our hearts, the Spirit of God does. Jeremiah 17:10 says, "But I, the LORD, search all hearts and examine secret motives" (NLT).

Turn off the distractions around you and set aside time to ask yourself, *What are the most consistent damaging thoughts I'm hearing in my own head, and when did they begin?* Then pray as David prayed: "Search me, God, and know my heart; test me and know my anxious thoughts. See if there is any offensive way in me, and lead me in the way everlasting" (Psalm 139:23–24). The answers you receive will advance your healing!

Give God Naming Rights

Psychologists say much of your self-esteem comes from what you believe the most important person in your life thinks about you. In other words, the weight of others' words varies depending on the place of authority they hold in your life. This is why when someone insults you in traffic, it's much less impactful in the long term than negative comments from your parents or spouse. The more you esteem someone, the greater the impact of their voice. This is why

Jacob was so quick to change his son's name. He recognized that the words from the boy's mother carried maximum weight.

Since the impact of someone's words is based on their level of authority, the essential step to undoing their negative effect is reassigning ultimate authority in your life to God. This is what Peter meant in 1 Peter 3:14–15: "Do not be terrified of them or be shaken. But set Christ apart as Lord in your hearts" (NET). In essence, Peter is saying, "Decide that God's voice will carry the most weight in your life."

Over the years, important people like your parents, peers, pastors, and spouse have said things to you that have shaped your life. But ultimate authority for declaring who you are belongs to one person alone—your heavenly Father.

You have the legal authority to name someone or something in two ways. First, you have naming rights over *what you create*, and second, over *what you purchase*. For example, Kayla and I had the right to name our kids because we created them. And in the case of my future boat (hey—a guy can dream!), I'll have the authority to name it because I purchased it.

> *Spiritually speaking, God has exclusive naming rights over your life because He created you and redeemed you through Jesus Christ.*

Spiritually speaking, God has exclusive naming rights over your life because He created you and redeemed you through Jesus Christ. First and foremost, God is the one who formed you in your mother's womb and determined your physical attributes, personality, mental acuity, and capacities (Psalm 139:13–16). He alone is responsible for your being here, therefore, He alone gets to name you.

Second and equally important, God has legal authority to name you and call you what you are because He purchased you out of the enemy's hands:

> You know that God paid a ransom to save you from the empty life you inherited from your ancestors. And it was not paid with mere

gold or silver, which lose their value. It was the precious blood of Christ, the sinless, spotless Lamb of God.

1 Peter 1:18–19 NLT

According to this passage, the only thing that adequately communicated how valuable you are to God was the life of His Son. In addition to His authorizing your birth on earth, He authorized your spiritual rebirth into His family. Thus God stands with your birth certificate in one hand and a bill of sale for you in the other, announcing to you, the enemy, and everyone else, "I alone have naming rights, and I've declared that you are My masterpiece" (Ephesians 2:10 NLT), My ambassador (2 Corinthians 5:20), the object of My love (Romans 1:7)!"

This revelation is life-changing, because the more weight you assign to God's voice, the weaker every other voice becomes. Eventually, you won't care what others have said about you, because you'll be certain about what God says about you.

Undo the Wrong Words with God's Word

Wounding words come from the mouths of many different people, but ultimately, they originate from the same source—our spiritual enemy. Every hurtful word you've ever heard was part of Satan's plan to assassinate your God-given purpose.

That said, it isn't enough to simply identify and acknowledge that what someone said was wrong. It must be detained and its impact undone. The only way to do this is to implement God's Word in its place.

Now, if you're wondering how to do that, you're in good company. A college student battling with feeling like a failure asked me that question not long ago. He knew the thoughts he was hearing weren't what God wanted for him, but he said it was much easier to believe the lie than fight against it. Essentially, he was asking, "How do I get God's thoughts to supersede how I feel?"

If you want to know the answer to that question, here's the Scripture I showed him: "No weapon formed against you shall prosper, and every tongue which rises against you in judgment you shall condemn. This is the heritage of the servants of the Lord" (Isaiah 54:17 NKJV).

Notice it doesn't say *God* will condemn what's said against you; it says *you* will condemn it. I believe this means God has provided the truth about who we are in His Word, but it's our responsibility to use that truth to condemn or undo the wrong things said against us. In short, you must use God's thoughts about you to trump the enemy's thoughts about you.

How to Make God's Thoughts Your Thoughts

Here's a practical, three-step exercise to help you release the power of Isaiah 54:17 in your life:

1. *Write down the wrong thought.* You say, "But, Joe, I thought we're not supposed to dwell on the wrong said. So we should just ignore it, right?" That approach is popular but not biblical. The Bible doesn't teach denial. It doesn't say to deny sin if you struggle with it. It says to confess it, which means to acknowledge it's there and agree with God that it's not His plan for your life. This is the difference between positive thinking and scriptural thinking. Positive thinking denies the problem. Scriptural thinking acknowledges the problem and declares God's grace supersedes it.

2. *Write down what God says in His Word.* You don't have to guess how God feels about you. He's made it clear in Scripture. One of the most powerful things you can do is learn to complete this sentence: "God says I am . . ." When you and I address how we feel with what Scripture says, something powerful happens: one by one, lie after lie comes down in our minds and is replaced by truth.

3. *Then review what you've written until the truth of who you are is rooted in your mind.* The result of your writing may look something like this:

- "I feel inadequate right now, but God says I'm more than a conqueror." (Romans 8:37)
- "I still feel broken, but God says in Christ I'm complete." (2 Corinthians 5:21)
- "I've made a lot of mistakes, and I still struggle with sin, but God says I'm forgiven and free." (Ephesians 1:7)

In a process this intricate, it's tempting to gain a measure of peace and then settle before finishing the work of renewing your mind. But my prayer is you won't stop! That you work God's Word into your life until every lie is repealed. Let's face it. You have to live with you. You spend more time with yourself than with any other human being, and if your thoughts are wrong, nothing else can be right. So don't stop until Scripture rules your subconscious.

Claim What God Has Said by the Way You Live

To settle who you are, it's not enough to receive Christ; you must also believe all He declares over you. Receiving Christ is how you secure *eternity*. Believing all He says about you is how you secure *identity*. This is a distinction many miss, and it's why James 1:22 says, "Don't just listen to God's word. You must do what it says. Otherwise, you are only fooling yourselves" (NLT). To claim what God has said about you, you must decide to wear it daily and discard what others say.

The year I turned nineteen was pivotal for me. I knew I was called to local church ministry, but I had no idea how to proceed. When I spoke to my pastor about it, he said, "That's not what I see for you. I think you should become a teacher or go into business." This was his way of saying my temperament or gifts didn't fit the typical mold for a pastor, and he was right. I couldn't sing, I didn't like working with kids or students, and I wasn't a charismatic communicator. His words simply reinforced what I already thought, and they entrenched the belief that I didn't have what it took to pursue my calling.

Receiving Christ is how you secure eternity. Believing all He says about you is how you secure identity.

For the next year I watched as many friends became pastors and received great ministry opportunities. I, on the other hand, had no direction and started considering alternative pursuits.

Then one Sunday as I was leaving the local church I attended while in college, an elderly man named Boyd England stopped me. He'd been a pastor and educator, and in his retirement he still provided Christian counseling for those who couldn't afford it. He was respected by everyone and embodied what a retired ministry leader should be.

As he pulled me aside, he asked about my classes and how I liked living away from home. Our conversation carried on for a few minutes, but as it was ending, he adopted a more serious tone. He stepped closer, placed his hands on my shoulders, and said, "Joe, I just have to say that you may not see it, but I see a pastor in you."

I was shocked by his words because I'd never told him a desire to pastor was in my heart. I immediately started trying to tell him how unlikely that was, but he interrupted me. "Listen," he said, "I know what I'm talking about. You are a pastor if I've ever seen one."

Something in me shifted. I went home thinking, *Could that be true? Maybe what I've been believing is wrong.* And with his words now imprinted on my heart, I decided to receive them as truth. I knew I needed to act on what he said, but how could I act like a pastor before I was a pastor? The best idea I could come up with was to wear a suit to church. I rarely wear suits today, but back then, every pastor did. So that's what I did although I had nowhere to preach and no title. For two years, I wore a suit every Sunday until I finally became what I wore.

Of course, suits aren't required to work at a church, but I needed a new mindset. Accordingly, God used an outfit to give me a better outlook.

How about you? Are you stuck, wrestling with self-defeat, and still wounded by words spoken to you—especially if they came from someone in the church? Realize that God has provided healing through His Word. It's time for you to claim it by getting your mind and your mouth in line with what He said. Today is the perfect day to shed those painful words and start wearing the plan God has for your life.

Heavenly Father, in the moment, I acknowledge that You have exclusive naming rights over my life. Therefore, I choose to believe what You say about me over what others have spoken about me. Please give me the persistence to tear down every defeating thought and replace it with Your truth until my mind is renewed. Amen.

11

Unresolved Conflict

I heard a story about an airline employee tending to an enraged passenger at the ticket counter. As the man complained about airline policies and peppered the attendant with insults over the job he was doing, the employee remained calm and pleasant. To the shock of those in the line, he kept smiling and never pushed back.

When the passenger's check-in was complete, he stomped away toward his gate. The lady next in line came forward, gently leaned over the desk, and said to the employee, "I'm so sorry you had to endure that. But I'm impressed with your level of self control. How did you stay so calm and kind?" The employee grinned and said, "Ah, that's easy. I just kept thinking about how he's going to Chicago but his bags are going to Nicaragua."

Clearly, conflict is a fact of life. Wherever there are two people, disagreements are inevitable because at some point what one wants the other opposes. This is true in marriage, on teams, and in friendships. While this isn't a new revelation, for some reason we seem to be caught off guard when conflict arises within the church.

I once heard someone say where there's more than one person in any room, you'll find two things: politics and conflict. In my experience that's true! Whether it's leaders who have opposing views for how a ministry should be done, members at odds over something that was said, or someone with hard feelings because of how a situation was handled, fights in faith communities happen because imperfect people are present.

So the question isn't *if* you'll experience conflict; it's whether you know how to handle it in a healthy way when it comes.

Carry or Confront?

Dr. Fred Garmon, who founded LeaderLabs, has trained over five thousand local and executive leaders in faith communities. In his research, Dr. Garmon has also determined that conflict is the "most dominant problem Christian organizations face":

> And while the corporate world gets training on how to deal with and manage conflict, with tremendous results, the Church continues to avoid it, with hopes that it will simply go away. In fact, my research shows among particular organizations and denominations, avoidance is the number one mode we choose, with collaboration being the last mode we choose. In other words, we are best at the worst possible choice, and worst at the best possible choice.[1]

If you've been part of the faith community for any amount of time, I think you'll agree that as Christ-followers, we're often untrained in how to resolve conflict. But that makes no sense! Not learning how to handle conflict in church is like not learning how to use scuba gear on a deep-sea dive. In the short term, you'll be miserable, and there is no long term, just a tragic end.

Jesus said, "It is impossible that no offenses should come" (Luke 17:1 NKJV). Although we can't choose whether people offend us, we can choose where offense takes us. Let me explain. When an offense takes place, you get to choose whether to *carry* it or *confront* it. When you confront it, you're choosing to resolve the issue with the other person. When you carry it, you're choosing to not include the other person and instead keep the offense with you.

Now, here's what you may not realize: both choices come with a level of discomfort, but the duration of the discomfort differs. The discomfort of confronting someone is short-lived because it most often brings resolution. But the discomfort from carrying the offense can last years because you'll experience resentment, impairing your emotions and faith. This means your choice to either carry or confront is really a choice to experience pain or peace.

I have no doubt that you agree with the logic of my explanation. But when it's applied to the active conflict you share with someone, logic fades and your emotions become your filter. That may be the single greatest reason we have unresolved conflict—we're not following God's wisdom but being led by our feelings.

Neither Blame nor Avoidance Is Effective

According to psychologist Robert Plutchik, humans can experience over thirty-four thousand unique emotions.[2] I'm not sure of the exact number, but when it comes to conflict, I think with all the emotions we experience, we're usually led to one of two places: blame or avoidance.

By blame, I'm referring to when the majority of your energy goes into assigning fault to the other person instead of pursuing resolution. This is when we "build a case" against someone and mentally review the facts again and again. The funny thing about blame is that it never makes us feel better.

Blame is giving someone the key to your happiness.

At its core, blame is giving someone the key to your happiness. Basically, you're saying, "I can't be happy unless you . . ." Do you really want to live with someone else controlling your ability to be happy? You could spend the rest of your life trying to assign levels of blame, but it would never do anything to change the problem. The fact remains, no one has ever blamed his or her way into a solution. Blame is a waste of effort and energy.

What about avoidance? I'm referring to when we choose to go silent, sweep the offense under the rug, or quietly quit the relationship. The problem with avoidance is that it addresses the situation only on the surface. You can change routines or schedules, even find a new church or job, but these actions won't unburden you. Out of sight, out of mind doesn't mean something has been moved out of your heart. Avoidance is often nothing more than a decision to be miserable somewhere else.

Unresolved Conflict Causes Us to Miss Out on God's Best

Anytime our emotions make our decisions, we miss what God intended. That's the core warning behind Proverbs 25:28: "Losing self-control leaves you as helpless as a city without a wall" (CEV). In essence, this writer is saying, "A life without self-control is a life in danger of losing God's best." I've learned that anytime I lose control of my reactions, I lose. I may lose influence, a friend, my job, my health.

Or even my faith.

To you, that may seem like hyperbole. You may think your faith is unaffected by your relationships, but it is affected. Above all, unresolved conflict becomes a ceiling to our relationship with God. Consider what 1 John 4:20 says: "If anyone says, 'I love God,' and hates his brother, he is a liar; for he who does not love his brother whom he has seen cannot love God whom he has not seen" (ESV). It doesn't get much clearer than that. It's impossible for you to love God and loathe someone!

Holding on to offense will cause your spiritual growth to stop. It may feel as though you have a broken faith, but you're dealing with a broken relationship. No matter how much of God's Word is regularly planted in your heart, it won't grow in the soil of resentment. Likewise, it doesn't matter how passionately you worship, how often you serve, or how much you give, because unresolved conflict is undoing God's best in your life.

I've sat with countless people who've been at odds with someone, and here's the one thing I always tell them: "To live with peace in the future, you have to make sure you do everything possible to live in peace with others in the present."

I'm not blind to the fact that sometimes relationships end and problems are too big to solve. Resolution doesn't always mean the relationship is restored to what it was before

Holding on to offense will cause your spiritual growth to stop.

the offense. It just means I did everything in my power to ensure the offense was addressed and unable to evolve into resentment.

Five Keys to Resolving Conflict

Thankfully, Jesus spoke directly to this issue and told us how to confront those with whom we're offended. In Matthew 18:15 He said, "If another believer sins against you, go privately and point out the offense. If the other person listens and confesses it, you have won that person back" (NLT).

In this verse, Jesus gives us five keys to ensuring we do all we can to resolve conflict and return to peace.

1. Ask God for help.

Notice the first thing Jesus mentions is "another believer." The implication is that He assumes that, as believers, we're viewing the conflict through spiritual eyes. This is vital, because to move forward with the steps Jesus is telling us to take, we need to operate in the mind of Christ (1 Corinthians 2:16).

You should always talk to God before you talk to the person with whom you're in conflict. Unfortunately, this is most often the step we skip. Usually, we talk to friends or family, trying to get them on "our side" before we pray. By doing so we end up gossiping, instead of gaining God's help. Prayer is talking to God before we talk to anyone else because He can do what no one else can.

Praying first honors God and enables us to receive two essential qualities needed for dealing with disagreements: His love and His wisdom. Our capacity to genuinely love someone doesn't come from our feelings but from God. Scripture says, "Dear friends, let us love one another, for love comes from God" (1 John 4:7).

Please realize that your relationships will be empowered either by you or by the Holy Spirit. It's a decision you must make and one of the most important ones. If you're the power behind your relationships, then your kindness, love, mercy, and patience are limited. But if you allow the Holy Spirit to empower them, everything He has is made available to you. That means you have an unlimited supply of love, mercy, kindness, patience, and everything else. As you put God first and regularly spend time with Him, He regularly refills what your relationships need.

Additionally, when you pray, you'll gain new insights into how to approach the situation. Think about it. God made the person you're in conflict with, and He made you. Therefore, He's the *only one* who knows what you both need and how to resolve what's wrong and make the relationship work. So make praying to God your first response, not your last resort.

2. Take initiative.

Chances are if you have unresolved conflict in your life, you're waiting for the other person to make the first move. You're waiting for them to send you a message, invite you to talk, admit where they were wrong, or apologize. And you're waiting because you don't want to go first.

Strangely, we like to be first in fantasy football, checkout lines, and out of the church parking lot on Sunday mornings. Easily, 75 percent of the fights my kids have are about being first. But I've noticed that few people fight to be the first to resolve a relationship that's broken.

This brings us to the second point in Matthew 18:15—the fact that Jesus tells us to "go" to the other believer. Rather than wait for them to come to you, you're to take initiative, be proactive, and go to them. This aspect of Jesus' instruction reveals that conflict is seldom resolved accidentally.

Do you know what cancer is? In simplistic terms, it's when a group of cells that used to be in harmony with all the other cells begin operating in opposition. What's interesting is that your body is made up of more than thirty trillion cells, but it takes only a few opposing cells to destroy it.

Unresolved conflict is like cancer in our lives. That's why Ephesians 4:2–3 passionately instructs us to "be completely humble and gentle; be patient, bearing with one another in love. Make every effort to keep the unity of the Spirit through the bond of peace." The tone of this passage isn't that of friendly advice or a casual suggestion. It's the writer shouting, "Do whatever it takes to stay in unity and preserve peace!" That's the same attitude you'd have if you learned you had cancer. You wouldn't "give it time" to heal itself. You'd take initiative before it got worse.

I encourage you to set a time and place to have a conversation with the person on the other side of this conflict—and do it today. Pick a time when you're both most likely to be at your best. Choose a quiet place that will allow you to concentrate, where you won't be interrupted, you can talk honestly, and your emotions can come out.

The most important part of taking initiative is that once you sit down together, you go first in confessing what you did to contribute to the conflict. Jesus told us this in what's called the Sermon on the Mount:

> Why do you look at the speck of sawdust in your brother's eye and pay no attention to the plank in your own eye? . . . You hypocrite, first take the plank out of your own eye, and then you will see clearly to remove the speck from your brother's eye.
>
> Matthew 7:3–5

Conversations that end in resolution begin with admitting, not accusing. I grasp that the other person may be 99 percent responsible for the wrong, but I'm asking you to begin by admitting the 1 percent you're responsible for. Do it because it displays humility, and humility opens the other person's heart, attracts God's grace, and repels the enemy's voice.

3. Be clear and kind.

Once the conversation has begun, point out the offense as Jesus instructed. That means focusing on attacking the problem, not the other person. You're not there to rip them apart; you're there to remove misunderstanding or mistreatments limiting a healthy relationship.

In the heat of conflict, too often we get off track with insults instead of keeping our focus on the issues. To avoid this, take time to gather your thoughts beforehand so you can communicate them clearly. Rather than focusing on what the other person did, focus on how their actions made you feel. For example, you can say, "When I hear things like [fill in the blank], I'm frustrated. And when I don't get [fill in the blank], I feel devalued."

The Bible says to "speak the truth in love" (Ephesians 4:15 NLT). This is the key to handling conflict properly and effectively. You may be able to tell the truth, but if it's not in love, then you're just using the truth as a weapon to hurt someone.

In Revelation 12:10, Satan is called the "accuser of our brothers and sisters." He's a nitpicker and a constant critic. When we're insulting, we amplify his voice in our relationships. Could your relationships be broken because you're tearing down other people? In all my years of counseling, I've never heard a wife say, "Joe, what really helped me and made me change for the better was when my husband started cursing at me. That did so much for me."

You'll never insult your way to a better marriage, nor will you belittle your way to more obedient children. And being critical won't win you more influence. You can't get good results with a bad attitude.

I like the way Pastor Rick Warren says it: "Truth without love is resisted; truth wrapped in love is received."[3]

4. *Listen attentively.*

Do you know why people raise their voices in the heat of conflict? Because they don't feel heard. This is why James instructed believers to be "quick to listen" (James 1:19). Listening is essential if you want to navigate disagreements.

Listening is also called *paying attention* because it costs you your agenda, preferences, and pursuits. It's when you stop for someone else, look them in the eye, and ask, "What do you want me to understand?"

I think it's interesting that today Christians are known for wanting to get their point across, but Jesus was known for asking questions. In the Gospels we see Him ask 307 of them. He obviously understood the power of listening. And He knew our asking a question makes a great statement about how we value the other person.

5. *Aim to win the person, not the argument.*

Often, the "win" of healthy confrontation isn't fixing the issue but sharing how we feel, releasing any hard feelings, and moving forward together. We have to acknowledge that while some issues can be fixed, not all of them can. We're all different in our experiences, views, and passions, and sometimes we just won't agree. But remember, the goal is not to win an argument; it's to not lose the person.

I've come to believe it's always more rewarding to resolve a conflict than to dissolve a relationship. Indeed, there's something more valuable at stake than getting my way, and it's revealed as we read a bit further into Matthew 18. Jesus' comments on conflict are often said to be contained in verses 15–17, but I believe they continue through verse 20.

First, look at what Jesus said in verse 18: "I tell you the truth, whatever you forbid on earth will be forbidden in heaven, and whatever you permit on earth will be permitted in heaven" (NLT). Although this appears to have left the topic of conflict and begun a discourse on prayer, read the next two verses: "I also tell you this: If two of you agree here on earth concerning anything you ask, my Father in heaven will do it for you. For where two or three gather together as my followers, I am there among them" (Matthew 18:19–20 NLT).

Clearly, Jesus didn't finish the topic of conflict in verse 17 but continued in an attempt to show us how resolving conflict is tied to releasing God's power in prayer. Essentially, Jesus was saying, "When you hold on to relational conflict, you lose spiritual power." That makes sense, because we can't come into agreement with someone we're against. That's why the New Testament warns that treating our spouse poorly will result in our prayers being hindered (1 Peter 3:7).

Are you beginning to see why the enemy has worked so feverishly to keep unresolved conflict in the church? He knows we'll have power if we make peace!

Resolving Conflict Releases Power

Are you waiting for God to do something specific in your life? What if it hasn't happened yet because He's waiting for you to resolve a conflict between you and someone else? I understand the issues are legitimate and the frustration is significant, but is it worth missing out on what God has for you? Focus on the fact that the quicker you resolve the conflict, the quicker God releases power.

You may be thinking, *But things are too bad, and they've gone unaddressed for too long. There's no hope.* I've felt that way, but time and time again I've seen that no relationship is so broken that God can't heal it.

Years ago I was speaking at a conference, and during one of my sessions, I talked about God's ability to heal broken relationships. At the end of the message, I invited people to respond by going to a leader so they could pray for restoration. Amazingly, nearly everyone in the room responded, so that time of prayer lasted quite a while.

I noticed a man standing on the side opposite me. Although I didn't know his story, I could see the pain he carried on his face. Then another man came up to him, hugged him, and began praying for him. It was a beautiful sight.

I leaned over and asked my host if he knew the backstory. He said, "Joe, that guy is our county sheriff, and the guy praying for him is Mike. Two years ago, Mike's brother was involved in an armed robbery, and he got into a shoot-out with the sheriff's department. It went on for some time until Mike's brother was shot and killed. Mike was crushed, and when the reports were released, they revealed that the bullet that ended his brother's life was fired by the sheriff, the man Mike's praying for. So what you're seeing is a miracle."

Just consider how the power of the Holy Spirit is so great that it can cause two men who have every reason to avoid or oppose one another to embrace. If He can do that for their relationship, what can He do in yours?

"But what if the other person involved doesn't respond well?" you ask. Then remember the promise in Proverbs 16:7: "When a man's ways please the LORD, He makes even his enemies to be at peace with him" (NKJV). Anytime you do what's right, you can trust God with the results.

The litmus test of spiritual maturity is not the absence of conflict but how we handle it. Conflict is *inevitable*. Resolution is *divine*. But God won't begin until you take a step of faith.

God, I recognize that You've called me to be a peacemaker, so I ask that You give me the humility and wisdom I need to resolve this conflict. Regardless of how the other person may respond, I want my ways to please You, so give me the courage to follow through. Thank You for going before me. Amen.

12

Loneliness and Isolation

A few years ago I decided to change up my exercise routine and start running. For years my workouts had centered around weightlifting, so I knew very little about distance running. Yet after the first week, I was already obsessed with the challenge to extend my distance and improve my time.

One day I noticed a pain in my right foot I'd never had before. It was irritating, but it didn't stop me from logging more miles. Eventually, though, that irritation became so debilitating that I could barely walk.

I visited my physician and learned I was suffering from plantar fasciitis. It's a condition where the thick band of tissue that runs across the bottom of the foot connecting the heel bone to the toes has become inflamed. I asked the doctor what was causing it, and he said, "It was most likely caused by your aggressive running routine." How strange. The very thing I was doing to get healthy was damaging my health.

I've seen something similar happen to people who've been hurt or seen others hurt in relationships. A common reaction to enduring pain or witnessing someone else's pain is to pull back from relationships. In our minds, we're preventing future pain and protecting ourselves from the unpredictable actions of others. What we thought would preserve our well-being, however, actually hurts it as the negative effects of loneliness take their toll.

More than ever, people are attending events with thousands, connecting online with millions, and yet living with a prevailing sense of isolation. Many of them are even sitting in churches, week after week, feeling left out, "looking from the outside in." It's the reason so many people claim churches are "cliques"—they feel disconnected and forgotten.

What makes this problem so challenging to solve is that no one sets out to be lonely. It's no one's goal or dream to live without significant relationships. It happens unintentionally:

- *Loneliness is a reaction to fear.* We've been burned by someone in the past, and the effects still linger. So we vow to never let it happen again, erect walls, and refuse to let anyone get close. We do this without realizing walls keep out both the bad and the good.

- *Loneliness is a byproduct of busyness.* We say, "I'd love to have closer relationships, but there's just so much going on. Maybe I'll have more time to invest when things settle down." But things never settle down. Weeks become months, and months become years of isolation.

- *Loneliness is a symptom of our social media world.* Although we have more likes and more followers than ever, we feel more alone than ever, and it's because social media has given us a false sense of connection. I observe what's going on in your world, and you observe what's going on in mine, but we never really enter each other's world. Our relationship remains on a surface level, leaving us connected but not invested.

We Were Created to Do Life Together

Each of these realities runs against the fact that we were created to be in life-giving relationships. God didn't design a single personality type or temperament to lead an independent life. When He made each of us, He installed a need for others.

This is made clear in the first two chapters of the Bible. In the creation account, each time God spoke something into existence, He then announced His approval of it. Scripture tells us that after the creation of the land and sea, the sun and moon, and the birds and fish, "God saw that it was good." Again and again, He created something and said it was good—*until* He created man.

Upon seeing man, who was created in His image, "the LORD God said, 'It is not good for the man to be alone'" (Genesis 2:18). Many people think the Bible is concerned only with the problem of sin, but here we see the first problem in the world wasn't sin. It was *isolation*.

The first problem in the world wasn't sin. It was isolation.

In His wisdom, God knew the damage of disconnectedness, and our scientific studies continue to affirm this. Dr. Julianne Holt-Lunstad, a Brigham Young University professor of psychology and neuroscience, analyzed data from 148 different studies worldwide. She found that a lack of significant social connection carries a risk similar to smoking up to 15 cigarettes per day, is twice as harmful as obesity, and is comparable to the lethalness of alcoholism."[1]

Now, I'm no doctor, but according to this research, it appears it's better to eat junk food with friends than exercise alone!

Relationships are literally life-giving. I realize this may be a hard pill to swallow considering the damage you've endured at the hands of others. There's no pain like being left out, misunderstood, betrayed, or discarded by someone with whom you shared your heart. And the more I'm around people, the more even I am tempted to move far away from everyone and live with God off the grid!

That sentiment has become common for people who've experienced church hurt. They say, "All I need is God," but that goes against what God said in Genesis 2:18. Before sin entered the world, nothing existed to impair the relationship between God and man. Yet God called Adam's aloneness "not good."

As much as we need God, He didn't design us to be in relationship with only Him. He designed us to be in relationship with each other. Therefore, He wants us to fight through the dysfunction, persist in extending forgiveness, and not give up on the concept of doing life with others.

God's Goodness Is Delivered Through People

To incentivize this design, God has chosen relationships as the primary delivery system for His goodness. Have you ever stopped to think about how much God does in your life through people? To recognize this truth, you need look no further than the concept of spiritual gifts. In 1 Peter 4:10 we read, "Each of you should use whatever gift you have received to serve others, as faithful stewards of God's grace in its various forms."

Throughout the New Testament, we read how God deposited spiritual gifts in every Christ-follower. Nearly thirty are listed, and they supply a wide array of assistance. Some of these gifts provide practical help, like administration, teaching, or needed resources. Other gifts display God's supernatural power of healing, miracles, and prophetic insight. Each gift is an expression of God's goodness toward the recipient, but it's delivered through people.

This means when God wants to encourage you, He does it through someone with the gift of encouragement. When God wants to teach you, He does it through a person with the gift of teaching. When you're desperate for direction, God guides you through someone with a gift of knowledge.

You may be thinking, *Wow! I'd love to experience those gifts, but they seem to be missing. How can I find and benefit from them?* The gifts are in God's people, which prompts me to ask whether you're in relationship with God's people—His church. God's power increases in your life as your involvement with His people increases.

Your Friends Can Be a Pipeline for God's Power

A powerful example of how the faith of friends can be a pipeline for God's power is found in the biblical account of a man who'd spent his life paralyzed on a mat. Imagine what his existence must have been like, unable to work or even feed himself in the ancient world with no government agencies, healthcare systems, or nonprofit organizations. And sadly, confined to that mat, this man who needed Jesus had no way to get to Him.

That is, until his friends showed up and picked him up. Mat and all, they carried their immobile buddy to Jesus. And their persistence paid off, because when Jesus saw the paralyzed man, He said, "'Get up, take your mat and go home.' Then the man got up and went home" (Matthew 9:6–7).

What I find most interesting is the statement in verse 2 that says, "Jesus saw their faith." Meaning, Jesus didn't comment on the paralyzed man's faith but on the faith of his friends. His friends' faith became the conduit for his miracle! While we can learn many lessons from this story, the greatest is this: no matter what's working against you, nothing is more powerful than having godly friends who are for you! The fact that this guy had no strength—and no money or education, let alone status—made no difference. He chose the right friends, and that was enough for God to transform his life.

Maybe you feel like you have no strength because this season has been so limiting that you feel your future is paralyzed. You see no way to pick up the pieces because your situation feels too overwhelming. I have good news.

You don't have to carry the load alone, because God is with you. And if you let Him, He'll transform your situation through the right people. Your only responsibility is to step out of isolation, push past excuses and your trust issues, and *choose* to prioritize and pursue right relationships. God's power in your life will increase as your involvement with His people increases. Though this experience has seemed to paralyze you, I believe you're going to walk into a better season!

How Connected Are You with Others?

Undoing the effects of isolation begins with being honest about where you are. In my experience, we all tend to overestimate the quality and quantity of the relationships we have. But nothing brings an overestimation back to reality like answering several questions honestly.

Take a moment to assess the landscape of your relationships by asking yourself the following questions and answering them with a yes or no.

- *Do I have one or more friends with whom I regularly share a meal?*
- *If I receive good news, do I have a friend with whom to celebrate?*
- *Do I have a friend I trust enough to share a secret with?*
- *When a situation becomes overwhelming, do I have at least one friend I can comfortably talk to?*
- *Am I in relationship with someone who can bring up my short-comings and I can receive their feedback without offense?*
- *Do I have a friend I know regularly prays for me?*

If you can't answer most of these questions with a yes, you're not as genuinely connected as you need to be. This means it's time to get serious about pursuing the God-ordained relationships He has for you.

Four Types of Friends You Need to Pursue

Too often our relationships are randomly added to our lives. That's how we end up with "friends" who drain or discourage us. Proverbs 12:26 says, "The righteous choose their friends carefully, but the way of the wicked leads them astray." This tells us relationships are too important to be left up to chance. We need to intentionally pursue connecting with people who are life-giving and bring out the best in us. Personally, I think we should all be on the lookout for these four types of friends:

1. *Friends who will encourage you*

A couple of years ago, I sat in my office across from a police officer who was struggling to keep his mind clear and his heart clean. Due to the nature of his job, nearly all his interactions were negative, and he expressed a temptation to quit because he just couldn't take it anymore. As I listened to him, I sensed the Holy Spirit prompting me to tell him quitting wasn't the answer, because once negativity is poured into us, it doesn't just evaporate. Instead, the toxic feelings in his heart would follow him to his next job. He needed to counteract the negative being poured by spending time with encouraging friends.

You see, again, negativity doesn't just disappear. It must be displaced. A heart filled with discouragement must be flushed out with encouragement. I believe that's why the Bible says, "Encourage one another daily . . . so that none of you may be hardened by sin's deceitfulness" (Hebrews 3:13). Notice it says we need encouragement *daily*. I believe this is God's plan to help us deal with the hardening effects of difficult people, a broken world, and spiritual opposition. Encouragement is so much more than saying something nice—it's a spiritual transaction.

Chances are you have a device in your home that's voice-activated. It could be your phone, a TV, or even a vacuum. What sets it apart from other devices is that its capacity is connected to your voice. You have to speak for it to achieve something.

An engineer didn't come up with that technology—God did. He's hardwired us to respond to the voice of another believer's encouragement. We're often blind to our potential and wide-eyed to our limitations, so we need the voices of other believers regularly encouraging us to activate our gifts and achieve all God has destined us to do.

Now, you may be thinking, *Who wouldn't love an encouraging friend? It's just so hard to find one!* And you're right. There seems to be a plethora of discouragement and a lack of encouraging people. But I have a solution. The way to find an encouraging friend is to become an encouraging friend. Remember, birds of a feather flock together. When you give encouragement, the law of sowing and reaping kicks in. You'll harvest encouragement when you plant encouragement.

Make it a goal this week to increase your encouragement of others. It's as simple as harnessing the power of your mouth to announce God's heart of love to people. As you do, I believe you'll attract encouraging people—or draw encouragement out of the people you're already around.

2. *Friends who will protect you*

One of the most unifying qualities of humanity is that we all have blind spots, and without someone else's eyes, we ignore, excuse, and even rationalize them away. In a way, we're all like the man on a diet who drove past Krispy Kreme and said, "God, if it's Your will for me to have a donut, let there be an empty parking space near the door." Sure enough, the fifth time he circled the lot, God's will opened up a space.

Life is not a game you play alone if you want to win. You need partners. Organizations like Alcoholics Anonymous and CrossFit have figured this out, but for some reason many Christians believe they can go without and keep everyone at arm's length. The result is that many churches are filled with people struggling in secret.

One of the greatest gifts you'll ever receive is a friend who will be honest with you. Someone who'll say, "I love you too much to let you compromise God's plan for your life." Of course, for that person to be honest, we have to give them permission to speak freely. And we do that by asking for their help, one of the most difficult things to do. It requires humility and pushing past feelings of weakness, broken trust, shame, and the concern of burdening others.

The truth is those concerns are legitimate, and there's a risk to each one. But I believe if you compare the risk of being vulnerable to the risk of remaining blind and never experiencing all God has for you, you'll conclude that the risk of vulnerability is worth it. I also believe that's why Solomon, the wisest man to ever live, wrote, "A person standing alone can be attacked and defeated, but two can stand back-to-back and conquer. Three are even better, for a triple-braided cord is not easily broken" (Ecclesiastes 4:12 NLT).

According to Solomon, some victories are possible only by trusting someone enough to cover the areas of our life we can't see. The question is who has your back. If you're drawing a blank, it's time to ask for help.

3. Friends who will laugh with you

One thing that gets on my nerves is the perception that assumes the more spiritual you are, the less fun you have. Holiness doesn't equal being humorless. As C. S. Lewis said, "Joy is the serious business of Heaven."[2] Unfortunately, joy is missing from many of our lives.

Research indicates children laugh or smile an average of four hundred times *daily*, but adults can muster only fifteen to twenty smiles a day.[3] What happens between childhood and adulthood to cap our capacity for joy?

I assume a few reasons include student loan payments and standing on a scale, but I also believe part of the problem is the people we hang around. Personally, I know if I'm not careful, I can spend all my time with people who generously share their anxiety, negativity, and complaints. But even if I limit my exposure to those who suck the life out of me, I also recognize I'm often not as present as I should be, and that causes me to miss meaningful moments.

One evening I was on the couch in our living room, dutifully studying for an upcoming message. At the same time, my kids were in the adjacent room having a dance party. I could hear the music thumping and the laughter increasing. Suddenly, I sensed the Holy Spirit telling me to put away my notes and go play with the kids.

This prompt challenged me because I'm so task oriented. But I sensed the Lord saying, *You can always write a message, but you won't always have this moment.* So under the inspiration of the Holy Spirit, I joined the dance party. I gave it all I had, and it didn't take long for my moves to move everyone to laughter. As I looked at each of my children's faces, I got this sense that I was in a holy moment. God was worshiped through our smiles as much as He's ever been worshiped in my study.

This experience taught me that to sense God's joy and have fun with others I must:

- *Prioritize good times.* How many times have you said to someone, "We need to get together," only to never follow through? In the Old Testament, God scheduled feasts for fun, and we need to schedule good times as well.
- *Be fully present.* We're a short-attention-span society. We've traded long conversations for social media posts, and it's reduced our capacity to celebrate. Turn off your phone, take a breath, clear your mind, and focus on the people present.
- *Celebrate others.* Did a friend just get a promotion, a clean bill of health, or make it through another semester? Then throw a party! Nothing makes people smile like being celebrated.

When we celebrate and laugh with others, we exercise the ability to see God's goodness in the simplest gifts. This act has a profound effect on our souls—like a prescription that clears up the infection of depression (Proverbs 17:22). Don't wait, put down your to-do list, invite some friends over, and have a dance party to the glory of God!

4. Friends who won't let you settle

Throughout your spiritual journey you'll have ups and downs. In some seasons, you'll have a natural hunger for God, but in others, your desire will fail. If you don't have people around who will spur you on, you'll settle for less than God's best.

That said, the fourth type of friend to look for is someone who isn't afraid to embody what I call a "holy irritation." I believe this is what God is referring to in Proverbs 27:17: "As iron sharpens iron, so a friend sharpens a friend" (NLT). These words seem poetic in a social media post, but they feel different in real life. When iron strikes iron, sparks fly. This means sometimes a great friend is irritating, provoking, and downright annoying. But when we need it most, God will use them to confront us and reignite spiritual hunger to keep it going.

This reminds me of when Kayla and I were on staff at an unhealthy church. It was plagued by power struggles and fights over preferences. I'm the type of person who pours myself into my work, so serving in such a fruitless and toxic setting really took a toll on me. For the first time, I experienced a bout of depression, and after serving in that environment for nearly four years, I desperately wanted to leave.

Then one day I got a call from another church about coming on staff. I was thrilled and felt like God had sent a lifeboat to rescue us. I didn't care about the salary or what the job description was; I just knew I wanted out, and the opportunity seemed like a great one.

Once Kayla and I visited the city and went through the interview process, the leadership team offered me the job. Although I asked for a couple of days to pray about it, I was already packing—I just didn't want to look unspiritual. During that period, a friend named Mark called, asking me about the process and what we wanted to do. As he listened, he could undoubtedly hear the excitement in my voice. But that didn't stop him from sharing his heart.

"Joe," he said after a pause, "I know how much you want to leave, but I don't think this is the right move. You could go and be fruitful, but I think God has something else that will be a perfect fit and unlock all He has put in you. I just don't want to see you settle."

As the conversation wrapped up, I was polite, but inside I was furious. I thought, *Some friend you are. You just want me to be miserable.* But over the next two days, Mark's words haunted me. Deep down, the Holy Spirit confirmed what he'd shared, and as you probably guessed, I passed on my lifeboat and chose to stay in the place I couldn't stand.

Ten months later, I received another call. Unlike when we received the first opportunity, God gave us the green light. And He's used this church to unlock gifts in me I never knew I had. I'm so grateful I had a friend who was willing to be my "holy irritation." Had Mark not been a true friend, I would have missed God's greater plan.

The quality of our lives is tied to the quality of our relationships.

Moving forward, you can be sure the enemy will offer you opportunities to settle for less than God's best, and they'll likely come when you're worn-out and frustrated. What friend will stand beside you and urge you not to settle?

Remember, the quality of our lives is tied to the quality of our relationships. I believe that, more than ever—and despite experiencing loneliness and isolation as a result of either your own choices, feeling pushed aside by some in the church, or both—it's time for you to reengage relationally and intentionally connect with the right people. After all, you may be one friend away from changing the course of your destiny.

God, I acknowledge You as my provider, and I'm asking that You provide the right relationships to end my loneliness. Please help me open up to new relationships as they cross my path, and increase my relational intelligence so that I can be life-giving to others. In Jesus' name, amen.

PART THREE

+

Reengaging
with Fresh Faith

13

Develop Staying Power

Other than choosing to follow Jesus, nothing has changed me more than having four daughters. Being their dad has softened me, made me a better listener—and opened me to a world I didn't know existed.

For example, one day Kayla asked me to help dress one of the girls by finding a pink hair bow to match her outfit. So I went upstairs, pulled out the containers of bows, grabbed a pink one, and took it to Kayla. When I handed it to her, she looked at me like I was crazy.

"Why did you bring me this?" she said. "I said a pink bow."

Confused and a little offended, I replied, "That is pink."

"No, it's a fuchsia."

In complete ignorance I asked, "What's a fuchsia?"

With a look of pity, Kayla spent the next several minutes enlarging my understanding of the color spectrum. Today, if you asked me to get you a pink bow, I wouldn't bring you a fuchsia, rose, blush, rouge, coral, peach, salmon, magenta, or bubble gum bow. I would bring you a pink one, because now I have greater perspective!

In this last section of the book, I hope to enlarge your perspective and give you a greater understanding of what it takes to move forward and healthily reengage in a faith community. For some of you, that means attending a service or event, and for others, it means opening your heart to the community where you already attend. But neither can happen if you don't see the church and yourself in a new light.

There's no doubt that the church has issues, but it also has some incredible benefits. For example, several studies show that those who attend church weekly have:

- A significantly lower risk of depression[1]
- Greater self-control and an elevated sense of meaning[2]
- Better grades and higher levels of education[3]
- Longer life expectancy[4]
- Better sex lives[5]

It's no wonder your spiritual enemy works so hard to destroy your relationship with the church. He doesn't want you to be happier, more efficient, smarter, healthier, or sexier!

To enjoy these benefits of a faith community, we need the right mindsets. And the first one you need is staying power.

Stay Planted Where God Placed You

If the Bible were expanded to include people through whom God has done remarkable things in the modern world, Tommy Barnett would certainly appear there.

As a pastor, he grew a church from just a few hundred people to more than ten thousand. As a leader, he's trained hundreds of thousands of pastors from around the world, enriched titans of industry, and counseled presidents. As an author, he's written more than ten books, including several bestsellers. And at age sixty, he founded the LA Dream Center, which feeds, houses, and restores tens of thousands of people ensnared in homelessness and addiction. This one Dream Center became a prototype for hundreds that followed in cities across the world.

Few people have made an impact like Pastor Tommy, so when I had the chance to glean from him, I jumped at the opportunity. The question I asked him was simple: "To what single quality do you attribute the fruitfulness of your life?"

Without hesitation, he said, "I didn't quit. I just stayed with it." So it wasn't about talent or luck; it was about staying planted.

As much as I respect Pastor Tommy, his advice wasn't original. The same sentiment is shared in Psalm 92:13–14: "Those who are planted in the house of the LORD shall flourish in the courts of our God. They shall still bear fruit in old age; they shall be fresh and flourishing" (NKJV).

God chose to reveal a huge portion about His nature and kingdom through the lens of agriculture. Think about this: God could have allowed the events of the Bible to unfold in the industrial revolution or the internet boom, but instead, He chose to reveal Himself to people who understood farming, gardens, and plant life. That could be why, in this modern age, we often miss what God is doing in our lives. After all, we aren't much of an agrarian culture anymore. Nevertheless, staying planted is how we grow a substantial faith.

Staying planted is how we grow a substantial faith.

Unfortunately, this quality is also foreign to our current way of life. We live in a culture that has very little staying power. It says, "If you don't like your marriage, just leave. If you don't like your job, just quit. If you don't like the situation, just pull out." This may be common practice, but it's creating a tragic problem, because to produce fruit you have to stay planted.

This is especially challenging for those of us who have experienced church hurt. Those memories are still powerful, and even if we've made progress on our healing journey, it's tempting to disengage the first time we sense the possibility of being hurt again.

Though you may see disengaging as a means of protection, I encourage you to fight that feeling and stay planted.

Now let me be clear. I am not instructing you to endure abuse or throw caution to the wind. There are predators out there. But if we're honest, we must admit that most of the time we aren't encountering predators, just people and all their dysfunctions—something we can never escape. Still, if you stay planted and work through conflict, forgive people's shortcomings, and trust the Lord, God will bring about His best in your life.

Four Reasons to Stay Planted

Picking up there, let's explore four reasons staying planted is crucial.

1. Staying planted allows the gardener to do a more significant work.

According to Scripture, God is the Master Gardener, and that's the mindset with which He approaches our lives. As a matter of fact, the first way God revealed Himself was as a gardener. The Bible says, "Now the LORD God had planted a garden in the east, in Eden; and there he put the man he had formed" (Genesis 2:8). Later, in verse 15, God struck up a partnership with Adam and put him in charge of His garden. I like to think of it as their starting Heavenly Father & Son Lawn Care, specializing in tree trimming and snake removal.

It's helpful to remember these two things about our God:

He loves the development process. The fact that He depicts Himself as a gardener from the beginning tells us He loves to watch things grow in our lives. Personally, I find nothing enjoyable about gardening. I don't like clearing the soil, planting seeds, or watering rows. I don't get excited when a little sprout pops up through the ground or when leaves fill every branch. Nothing about the development interests me, but God loves it—in all His creation, including you.

He enjoys observing every little step of your life. He loves watching you learn the smallest spiritual truths for the first time, and He loves seeing you take your first baby steps of faith. He also loves watching you make tiny choices to maintain your integrity.

This reality both challenges me and comforts me. It challenges me in that if I'm not much further down the road to maturity than when Christ first entered my life, God isn't as free to work in me as He wants. Yet it comforts me because it lets me know He's still actively at work. I'm not finished. I'm getting better, and my best days are ahead.

He desires our dependence. If you have a plant in your house, no matter what kind it is, it can't survive without you. It's dependent on you for water and to position it to receive sunlight. And just as the plant is completely dependent on you, God wants you to be dependent on Him.

In our culture, as you mature you become more independent and put increasing trust in your own abilities and wisdom. But in God's kingdom, as you mature you become more dependent on Him and put increasing trust in His abilities and wisdom. Here are two of the greatest Scriptures that express God's desire for our dependence on Him:

- Jesus said, "I am the vine; you are the branches. If you re-main in me and I in you, you will bear much fruit; apart from me you can do nothing" (John 15:5).
- And Paul wrote, "I can do all things through Christ who strengthens me" (Philippians 4:13 NKJV).

In John 15:5, the word *nothing* is a compound of the two words *no* and *thing*. So when we pair the meaning of this verse with Philippians 4:13, we see that without Jesus, we can do *no thing*, but through Jesus, we can do *all things*. I love that I don't have to focus on doing things. I just need to focus on giving Christ access to my life, and He does all things. Staying planted allows the gardener to do a more significant work.

It's true that an apple tree can grow apart from an orchard, but trees in the orchard grow to a greater stature because the gardener can access them more easily and frequently. So it is with our lives. You can have a relationship with Christ apart from the church, but Christ has so many more ways to access your life when you *are* part of the church.

2. Where you're planted determines what you take in.

The roots of a tree take in whatever is in the soil. The tree's potential is tied to its intake. Likewise, your potential as a believer is tied to your intake, and your attention serves as the roots of your life. Whatever dominates your attention grows. If all the bad news has your attention, *fear* grows. If comparison has your attention, *discontent* grows. If an offense has your attention, *resentment* grows. And if your to-do list has your attention, *stress* grows.

Sometime ago, Kayla and I were on a healthy eating kick. (I could give you the details, but the short of it was we ate like giraffes: all things green, nothing with flavor.) One day Kayla sent me to the store to pick up a few items. I was doing really well on the diet, but as I was grabbing the last thing she asked for, I saw a sign with the words *Ice Cream*.

I looked away, but my most direct route to the checkout lines was down that ice cream aisle. I figured it wouldn't hurt, but not taking a detour was a big mistake. The more ice cream I saw, the more I wanted some. My taste buds began to tingle, and my mind began to plot.

Suddenly, a little voice popped into my head and said, *Stay away.* Now, you may think that was the voice of the Holy Spirit, but I'm convinced it was my wife's, who somehow managed to access the sound system from miles away! Thankfully, I just shut my eyes, listened to the voice, and kept moving.

Here's my point: if you can control your attention, you can grow your faith.

One of the benefits of planting yourself in a faith community is that you're giving more of your attention to God's Word. You're shutting your eyes and ears to the world and listening to God's voice.

And don't forget, faith comes—or grows—by hearing the Word of God (Romans 10:17).

So many people are miserable because they think they need to grow themselves. That they have to change themselves. That they have to refresh themselves and force themselves to be fruitful. But none of that is true. The beauty of following Jesus is that we don't have to make ourselves grow. We just have to give Him more of our attention, and growth will happen naturally!

The Bible confirms this:

> Just as you accepted Christ Jesus as your Lord, you must continue to follow him. Let your roots grow down into him, and let your lives be built on him. Then your faith will grow strong in the truth you were taught, and you will overflow with thankfulness.
>
> Colossians 2:6–7 NLT

This passage is so encouraging! It tells me I don't have to push myself; I just have to plant myself in Christ. If I keep showing up and opening my heart to Him, over time I'll notice spiritual growth and maturity in every area of my life, including my parenting, my attitude, my thinking, and ultimately my behavior. As we plant our attention on Christ, He does the cultivating, and His power does the changing.

3. Where you're planted determines to whom you're connected.

Looking again at Psalm 92:13, it says, "Those who are planted in the house of the LORD shall flourish in the courts of our God" (NKJV). Notice it doesn't say "Those who *attend*." It says, "Those who are *planted*." There's a difference. You weren't designed to pop in and out of church, casually connecting here and there. You were designed for deep community in God's family. People who stay on the fringe of church life are too easily uprooted.

Have you ever seen the redwood trees in California? They're some of the largest trees in the world, towering over 275 feet into the air and measuring twenty-five feet in diameter. Many would assume these mammoth trees have extremely deep roots, but they don't. Their roots go down only six to twelve feet. And yet they rarely fall over. They can withstand strong winds, earthquakes, storms, and even prolonged flooding.

How can they remain standing for centuries with such shallow roots? The secret is their root system. Each tree's roots are intertwined with the roots of other redwoods. They grow very close together and are dependent on one another for support. So when the wind comes, it doesn't blow against a tree—it blows against the forest.

God designed you to intertwine with other believers. While you can't face cancer alone, you can face it together with fellow believers. By yourself, debt can cripple you and depression can defeat you. But they're no match against the united strength of the family of faith. Scripture reveals this again and again: the deeper you're in community, the more guaranteed your victory.

4. Where you're planted determines how fruitful you are.

God loves development and our dependence on Him, but more than anything He loves watching a single seed multiply. It thrills Him to see an apple become an orchard, an acorn become a forest, and a seed of faith in a person become a life of purpose.

When God grows you, He has more than you in mind. You're blessed to be a blessing. He saved you so you can serve others. As a matter of fact, the first instruction God gave humanity was to be fruitful and multiply (Genesis 1:28). Your life is meant to impact the lives of others, and if it's not, you haven't yet become what God designed you to be.

I love the way this is explained in Psalm 92:12: "The righteous shall flourish like a palm tree, He shall grow like a cedar in Lebanon" (NKJV). When we read about palm trees and cedars, we might not think much of them. But these trees were significant to the ancient Palestinians because of their unique characteristics.

Palm trees were common and used in everyday life to create things like baskets, rope, and even juice. Cedars, on the other hand, were exceptional. The ones from Lebanon were so famous for their strong wood and so superior that King Solomon imported them for the building of the temple in Jerusalem. Cedar was the material chosen to build a place for people to experience God's presence.

When God grows you, He has more than you in mind. You're blessed to be a blessing.

When you stay planted in God's house, you yourself become the place people experience His presence. You become the reason kids in a classroom discover God's presence. You become the reason people in the office experience God's character. You become the reason your neighbor experiences God's love.

Though each of us can serve others on our own, research shows most of us don't. In a study on the practice of charity and volunteerism in the US, researchers from Gallup reported that "Christians are more likely than those with no religious affiliation to report that they made donations and volunteered time."[6] So the people who make the greatest impact for good in the world are part of the local church, which means your life is more fruitful by being planted in God's house.

Today, many people transplant themselves from one church to another at the first signs of difficulty. But this can be harmful to your spiritual health.

Years ago, Kayla and I had some trees planted in our yard while we were out of town. When we returned, we didn't like their placement, so we wanted them transplanted to another area. But then I learned gardening experts warn against transplanting, because every time a tree is moved, its root system is stunted, and its growth potential is reduced.

May I tell you why so many people aren't where they want to be? Because they keep transplanting their lives. They begin attending church, but then they get busy. They dabble in reading the Bible, but then they get bored. They serve in a ministry for a little while, but when it's no longer convenient, they pull themselves up and transplant themselves back to their old life or to another pursuit. And every time they do, their roots are stunted, and their potential is reduced.

If you want to realize your potential and inherit all that God has planned for your life, determine today to be a person of staying power. Stay when it's not convenient. Stay when progress appears stalled. And stay despite difficulty. People with that attitude cause God to take notice and say, "I can do something in their life because they have staying power."

God, life is full of distractions and dysfunctions that tempt me to disengage, but I recognize that You reward faithfulness. Today, I ask that You renew a steadfast spirit in me—one that demonstrates patience, longsuffering, and Your character day in and day out. Amen.

14

Be Responsible
for Your Own Growth

When my son was in preschool, Kayla hung a decorative board on the wall to chart the kids' height as they grew. (This growth board was a point of contention in our house because she bought a scale to chart mine!)

The moment she hung that board, Sawyer became obsessed with getting taller. One night at dinner I noticed he was holding his vegetables in one hand, holding his nose with the other hand, and then forcing the food into his mouth. I knew he hated vegetables, so I asked him what he was doing.

He said, "I'm trying to grow."

I think many people feel like Sawyer: they're desperate to grow spiritually, but they're frustrated because they're not seeing results. Maybe by now you thought you'd understand the Bible better or enjoy prayer more. Maybe you thought you'd have grown out of certain struggles. Maybe you expected to have a clearer understanding of God's purpose for your life. But despite your expectations, you still haven't reached the stature you desire. After all this time, you're left asking, *Why am I not growing?*

After years of helping people chart a path for spiritual growth, I think the most widespread answer is that we're fast to blame and slow to take responsibility. In my opinion, these two realities limit your growth potential more than anything else, and I want to unpack both so you can remove the limits.

We're Quick to Blame

Blame is when we hold someone else responsible for where we are in life, and humanity has struggled with blame from the beginning.

The first two people God created were Adam and Eve. They were perfect people in a perfect place. The garden of Eden was theirs to enjoy, with only a single tree called "the tree of the knowledge of good and evil" off-limits (Genesis 2:17). One day in the form of a serpent, Satan convinced Eve to disobey God's instruction by eating the fruit of the forbidden tree. It wasn't long before Adam followed suit and God's perfect world was marred by sin.

You'd expect God to show up ready to punish Adam and Eve, but like any loving father, His first concern was for His kids. He came into the garden and found Adam and Eve hiding in shame, and then He talked to them about what happened:

> "Have you eaten from the tree that I commanded you not to eat from?" The man said, "The woman you put here with me—she gave me some fruit from the tree, and I ate it." Then the Lord God said to the woman, "What is this you have done?" The woman said, "The serpent deceived me, and I ate."
>
> Genesis 3:11–13

We don't know what God would have done if Adam or Eve had taken responsibility, confessed, and asked for forgiveness. Instead, each blamed the other, and great pain followed that decision.

Isn't it interesting that the first relational dysfunction in human history was one person blaming another? And we think after all these years we're enlightened, but this remains a problem. Many people blame their lack of growth on a lack of opportunity, a lack of access to resources, a lackluster leader, or mistreatment by an unloving peer. This drives people to repeatedly change churches, criticize leaders, tolerate their own resentment, and remain spiritually stagnant. But blame has never made any situation better.

Taking Responsibility Releases Growth

I know it may be hard to believe, but God has given you the ability to grow your own faith. And He's also given you the responsibility to do it, meaning you're exactly where you've led yourself to be. But most people never exercise that ability or take responsibility because they misunderstand how spiritual growth happens.

Jesus addresses this very issue in a story commonly referred to as the parable of the sower. He said there was a farmer who desired growth, so he went out to plant crops. In that culture they didn't plant a single seed and cover it up; they cast many seeds widely. And in this story, Jesus said the seed fell on four different places and had four different results:

- Some seed fell on a footpath where birds ate it before it could grow.
- Some seed fell on rocky soil where it initially sprang up, but a shallow root system caused it to fail.
- Some seed fell among thorns, and though it sprouted, it was eventually crowded out.
- And some seed fell on good soil, grew exponentially, and produced a significant harvest.

After hearing this story, Jesus' disciples said, "We don't understand your illustration. Can you explain it more clearly?" So Jesus took this natural example and explained the spiritual truths behind it:

The farmer plants seed by taking God's word to others. The seed that fell on the footpath represents those who hear the message, only to have Satan come at once and take it away. The seed on the rocky soil represents those who hear the message and immediately receive it with joy. But since they don't have deep roots, they don't last long. They fall away as soon as they have problems or are persecuted for believing God's word. The seed that fell among the thorns represents others who hear God's word, but all too quickly the message is crowded out by the worries of this life, the lure of wealth, and the desire for other things, so no fruit is produced. And the seed that fell on good soil represents those who hear and accept God's word and produce a harvest of thirty, sixty, or even a hundred times as much as had been planted!

Mark 4:14–20 NLT

Let's look at three truths concerning spiritual growth:

1. Growth begins with the seed of God's Word.

Giving has a purpose, serving is part of the journey, and godly relationships are vital, but let me be clear: there's no growth without a personal relationship with God's Word!

If you were to ask people to describe the Bible, some might say it's a catalogue of teachings, and others might say it's a record of ancient events. But those descriptions fall short of the true weight of God's Word. The Bible isn't "just a book." It's sixty-six different books written by more than forty people from all walks of life over fifteen hundred years ago. And despite incredible improbabilities, it's completely, thematically unified and prophetically accurate. How can this be?

There's no growth without a personal relationship with God's Word.

The apostle Paul explains the supernatural nature of Scripture: "God has breathed life into all Scripture. It is useful for teaching us what is true. It is useful for correcting our mistakes. It is useful for making our lives whole again. It is useful for training us to do what is right" (2 Timothy 3:16 NIRV).

Paul used the Greek word meaning "breathed out" to describe Scripture. When we speak, we breathe out. Therefore, the Bible is supernatural, because when God spoke out the content to the writers, His breath was on every word.

Wherever God breathes, significant things happen:

- He breathed into dirt and Adam came to life (Genesis 2).
- He breathed on the waters of the Red Sea and slaves were delivered to a new life (Exodus 14).
- He breathed on the top of poplar trees to guide David to victory over those who threatened his life (1 Chronicles 14).
- He breathed into the disciples, filling them with the Holy Spirit, and the church came to life (John 20).

And when we read Scripture, we allow God to breathe on our lives.

Scripture also leads to success. Planting God's Word in our hearts is how we prosper physically, emotionally, relationally, and financially. That's not my opinion; that's according to a Harvard study:

> The research examined respondents' scores on the Human Flourishing Index, which asks about people's "happiness & life satisfaction," "mental & physical health," "meaning & purpose," "character & virtue," "close societal relationships" and "financial & material stability." On the Human Flourishing Index as a whole, practicing Christians received an average score of 7.8 compared to 6.9 for non-practicing Christians and 6.7 for non-Christians.

Researchers, therefore, concluded that "scripturally engaged Christians flourish in every domain of human experience."[1]

In the natural, some seed planted is bad and never produces. But according to 1 Peter 1:23, every single verse of God's Word is imperishable, perfect, powerful, and able to prosper your life.

2. Growth has little to do with the sower.

Did you notice how little Jesus said about the one who sowed the seed? He placed *no* expectation on the sower, yet many people place *all* their expectation on the sower in their own lives. By sower, I mean the pastors, teachers, preachers, or people we receive from. If we're not careful, we fall into the kind of thinking that searches for the perfect sower: *I need someone with a specific sowing style. I need it to be funny and practical, but not so practical that it's not inspiring. But not so inspiring that it lacks depth. And it'd be great if they could sow it in thirty minutes or less.*

A consumer, self-focused mindset will kill your spiritual growth. As followers of Jesus, we don't shop for our church family or spiritual leaders. We ask God to plant us, and we respond to His leading.

The world has so many talented teachers and powerful preachers, but keep in mind that Jesus doesn't identify the sower other than saying he was "a farmer." I believe that's because the sower's style, message structure, decibel level, and social media prowess is irrelevant. The sower doesn't determine growth; the soil does.

3. Growth has everything to do with the soil.

Although the heading in your Bible may read Parable of the Sower, a more accurate description might be Parable of the Soil, because the soil determines the success of the seed.

You can have the most talented sower and great seed, but it doesn't matter if the seed falls on unwelcoming soil. This is why in Mark 4:13, before Jesus explains the meaning of the parable to the disciples, He implies that we must understand it because the condition of our hearts has more to do with our growth than any other factor.

This is a similar reality to anyone who's ever tried to get in shape. I've discovered it doesn't matter if I do CrossFit, cardio, or cycling, I still can't outwork a bad diet. The gym is a factor, and the movements are a factor, but nothing impacts the process like my diet. In a similar sense, you can't harvest from bad soil, and you can't grow with an unkept heart.

What's Needed for Growth?

So what can we do to prepare our hearts and propel our growth? Here's what we know according to Jesus' explanation.

Growth Requires Boundaries

The first soil Jesus described was a hardened footpath. In that day, many roadways were underdeveloped, so it was common for people to create their own path by walking through a field. Without fences or boundaries, over time the foot traffic packed down the soil of the field, making it impossible for seed to penetrate. In essence, Jesus was saying fruitfulness is impossible for the life without fences.

In order to grow, God's Word has to be able to germinate in your heart. But when we live without boundaries, the foot traffic of busyness, other people's expectations, and non-stop distractions have a way of packing down our hearts. The choice to not limit the traffic of your life is a choice to limit your faith.

Proverbs 4:23 says, "Above all else, guard your heart, for everything you do flows from it." The phrase *above all else* is another way of saying "give top priority to." Meaning, each day you should make time for God to speak to your heart a top priority. Why is the writer so emphatic? Because everything you do *will* flow from your heart: your parenting, your attitude, your decisions—everything.

I wonder if this is why this is the only soil in Jesus' description that attracts attention from our spiritual enemy (the bird stealing from it). Could it be that a life without boundaries is a primary target of the enemy because it's easy to keep barren?

I read an article about someone's trip to Sequoia National Park to see the massive trees I referenced in the chapter on developing staying power. When the writer entered the forest, he was surprised to find a fence around each tree. Turns out that sometime earlier, one of these massive trees mysteriously fell, shocking the forestry experts. They didn't understand why what appeared to be a healthy tree would suddenly collapse. But upon examination, they discovered the tree had fallen due to foot traffic. Over the years, park guests had walked on the root system, and unbeknownst to them, they were killing the tree.

What's true of the sequoias is also true of you and me. Without protection, our root system—our connection to God and His Word—will fail. And when it does, not only will we fail to grow, but we'll eventually collapse. If you want unlimited faith, you have to limit the foot traffic of life.

Growth Requires Honesty

When Jesus spoke about rocky soil, He wasn't talking about small pebbles; a farmer would remove those with a rake. He was referring to a limestone bedrock below the topsoil. This layer of rock was common to the region, and it had to be removed or the plants—though they quickly sprang up—would eventually die. Successful farmers knew there was no growth unless they addressed what was beneath the surface.

Today, many people put more emphasis on image than what's beneath the surface of their lives, resulting in a faith that has no depth and simply settles for checking a religious box. We say, "I went to church," or "I served at that event," or "I gave some money" and call it all good.

The problem is religious activity never brings about true change or satisfaction. To gain those, you have to allow the Holy Spirit to address the deep issues within your heart. Issues like the hurt you've been holding, what happened in that former relationship, the habits you've always excused, or the attitude you know is contrary to God's plan.

James 1:21 says, "Get rid of all moral filth and the evil that is so prevalent and humbly accept the word planted in you, which can save you." Notice the way to get rid of the issues under the surface is by accepting or planting God's Word in your heart. You will never find victory until you learn how to plant a verse in there.

Most people read God's Word so they can say they completed the task. But we plant God's Word in our hearts and activate its power when we meditate on it. *Meditation* is a word that usually catches people off guard. Their first thought is Eastern meditation, where you lie on a mat and empty your mind. But biblical meditation is different. It's when you lay open your heart and fill your mind with God's Word. It's the idea of keeping a verse or passage at the front of your mind throughout the entire day.

Simply focus your attention on a verse or passage to the point that it never leaves your mind. And as you do, the Holy Spirit will dig out issues, begin to exchange wrong thinking for His thinking, and begin removing the barriers that keep you from growing deeper.

Just try it. Pull up a verse like 2 Timothy 1:7: "God has not given us a spirit of fear, but of power and of love and of a sound mind" (NKJV). Then:

- On day one, simply read it.
- On day two, read it again and choose to think about it. What sticks out to you?
- On day three, read it again, and I bet you'll notice the Holy Spirit highlighting a place of fear you've buried. Maybe it's a fear about money or the future.
- On day four, read it again and think about God's power—how it's unlimited and available.
- On day five, read it again and focus on the fact that if God loves you, He won't leave you unprotected and He'll always provide.
- On day six, read it again and start surrendering the fear to God and declaring His promise of power, love, and a sound mind.
- On day seven, read it again, and my guess is you'll find your faith is growing. That's because now you haven't just read this verse, you've planted it in your soul.

Meditating on God's Word turns a simple verse into a significant victory!

Growth Requires Tenacity

Next, Jesus says some seed falls among thorns or weeds, meaning the soil's condition allowed for growth but the harvest was in jeopardy due to competing plants.

I think this is the spiritual state of most Christians' hearts. Their growth is slow and marginal because of so many competing agendas. Their heart is full of career pursuits, family priorities, hobbies, and financial goals. Individually, there's nothing wrong with any of those, but Jesus is making the point that, put all together, it's impossible to truly cultivate faith because the heart is so crowded.

Life never works when we just try to fit Jesus in. Jesus isn't added to our life; He *is* life! Many people try church, try prayer, and try faith and wonder why they aren't getting the results they desire. It's because Jesus isn't a hobby or casual connection. He's the King of kings and Lord of lords, and His kingdom and its blessings appear only in a life under His rulership.

Jesus isn't added to our life; He is life!

Next to the very first house Kayla and I owned, a neighbor planted a couple of bamboo shoots in his yard. But bamboo is one of the most invasive species on the planet. It spreads incredibly fast and chokes out other plants, and it didn't take long for it to spread to our yard. I'd cut it back, but it would grow back thicker. In desperation, I looked up how to stop it and discovered you have to dig down and sever every root. The job required only two things: time and tenacity, and your relationship with God requires the same two things.

"But, Joe," you say, "this is such a demanding season. I'm short on time." I understand. We have five children! Everyone is busy. But I recently read that the average person reads more than 265 social media posts, emails, and texts on their phone or tablet *every day*. Turns out we have time; we just have to redirect it.

In an effort to get our church to take spiritual steps, for years I kept lowering the bar, imploring people to read at least a chapter of the Bible a day. Then I lowered the bar to only one verse a day. Eventually, I was tempted to tell them to at least put the Bible under their pillow in the hope that osmosis would take effect. But one day in prayer, I sensed God correcting me for lowering the bar instead of calling people higher. That Sunday I publicly apologized and challenged everyone to dig into God's Word by giving it their full attention.

I'm giving you the same challenge today. Yes, you're busy, but nothing you're doing is more important than what you'll receive from the Word of God. Your job will pass away. Your hobbies will pass away. Streaming entertainment and social media will both pass away. In Mark 13:31, Jesus said even heaven and earth will pass away.

But God's Word will stand for eternity. The time you dedicate to Scripture is the most important time of your life because the benefits will last your entire life!

How to Get the Most from Scripture

Yes, you have time for Bible reading, but you may not know how to get the most from it. Allow me to share a format for success:

- *Set an appointment*—Instead of just trying to fit Bible reading in, choose a time when you can be consistent and at your best.
- *Select a reading plan*—Instead of randomly scrolling through Scripture, find a plan that a little more methodically takes you through what God has to say.
- *Read the day's passage slowly*—The goal isn't to "get through" your Bible reading; it's to plant God's Word in your heart.
- *Look up what you don't understand*—Too often, the first time we see a word we don't recognize or a concept we don't quite understand, we just stop reading and claim the Bible is too hard.

About that last point . . . You're more than capable and competent to understand the Bible. In this digital age we have more resources than any generation before. And most importantly, as a believer you've been given the mind of Christ and the Holy Spirit as your teacher. All you have to do is keep showing up, keep digging, keep searching, and keep reading. Your tenacity will increase your capacity.

If You Work the Word, the Word Works!

The last soil in Jesus' parable is a picture of the heart of someone who implements boundaries, approaches God's Word honestly, and keeps at it tenaciously. When Jesus' listeners heard Him say that type of heart should expect a 30-, 60-, or 100-fold harvest, their mouths no doubt dropped open in disbelief.

The average crop in Israel at that time was about 7-fold. Nobody had ever heard of 30-, 60-, or 100-fold. What Jesus was describing wasn't natural; it was supernatural! It's a reminder that when you do your part, God does His part. If you'll clear your heart, God will cause you to grow at an exponential rate.

Today, most people who meet Kayla are taken aback at how approachable and confident she is. But what they see isn't what she's always been. Kayla lived much of her early life debilitated by insecurity. I'm not talking about the struggle we all have from time to time. Kayla was crippled by comparison and the fear that she didn't measure up.

When Kayla and I were dating, on more occasions than I can count, over the phone she'd tell me she'd cried herself to sleep worried about disappointing people. It didn't matter what reassurances I gave her; she was in complete bondage. Maybe the most frustrating part was that no matter how much she prayed and no matter how many sermons she heard, she was still bound. Nothing seemed to help.

Out of desperation one day, I told Kayla that instead of my talking her through her fears every time she felt them rising, I'd give her a Bible verse to combat the disabling thoughts and then we'd get off the phone. For months she took that verse, read it again and again, poured out her heart to God, and let His Word rebuild her confidence until she felt peace.

Then one day when we were talking, a subject that would normally cause her to spiral came up. But instead of descending into the usual dark place in her mind, she just moved on in the conversation. This happened a few more times, and I realized it had been months since Kayla had said anything about her lack of confidence or shown any sign of anxiety.

Months became years, and years have become decades. What couldn't be healed by a relationship, medicine, or human effort was completely healed by the Word of God. Kayla took responsibility for her heart and growth, and she found the freedom she desperately wanted.

I wonder what freedom or blessing is on the other side of your taking responsibility for your own growth.

God, I'm ready to move from surviving to thriving! I want my faith to expand and my character to reflect Yours. Give me a fresh hunger for Scripture, focus to fight distractions, and the ability to understand Your ways. In Jesus' name, amen.

15

Embrace a Flexible Faith

The Greek philosopher Heraclitus said, "No man steps into the same river twice, for it's not the same river and he's not the same man." Whether that's the first time you've read his quote, or you remember it from a Philosophy 101 exam, we can all agree that change is a fact of life. But just because it's a fact doesn't mean we like it.

Change is a challenge for many people, and that seems to be especially true for those within the church. Over the years I've observed that the seasons that test a church family the most are when there's a change in leadership, style of ministry, or even décor. It's sad to admit, but some of the most ungodly conduct I've witnessed has been during debates about something like the color of the carpet in a choir room!

Ultimately, change is difficult because it disrupts, and those disruptions reveal deeper issues. Desires like:

- A *desire for control*. Part of our fallen nature is to rule over one another. Change brings conflict, because often it's one preference toppling another. And we all like our preferences.
- A *desire for comfort*. Why would people care so much about furniture or the color of a carpet? Because some of our most

significant spiritual experiences happened on that furniture or carpet. Like pieces in a museum, we want to keep styles, songs, and practices in place to maintain our treasured memories.

- *A desire for security.* The world is an unpredictable place, and we want the church to be a place of escape. That's why some refer to it as a sanctuary. But when things inside the church change as much as things outside the church do, we can feel unsettled.

In 2020, the entire world got a crash course in change through a pandemic. In a matter of days, how we traveled, worked, and worshiped was altered. As my own routines, comforts, and priorities were affected, I experienced a gamut of emotions that included fear, anger, confusion, and grief.

But eventually, I entered a reflective state of mind, and I remember asking God in prayer, *What are You trying to teach me in all of this?* In that moment, I sensed the Holy Spirit saying, "I'm teaching you to have a flexible faith. A faith that can bend when the load is heavy. A faith that can stretch when the wait is long. A faith that can remain in a world that takes unexpected turn after unexpected turn. A faith that can expand to receive all that I want to pour in!" From that season, then, I learned valuable lessons that continue to motivate me to maintain a flexible faith.

God Is Looking for Flexibility

Why is God looking for flexibility in us? I think for three reasons:

1. Flexibility is necessary to reach our full potential.

One of the most endearing things about God is that He fully loves us as we are while at the same time He knows what a project we are. He's not intimidated by our rough edges, but He's also not satisfied with leaving us in our current state. He's made His intentions known in Romans 8:29: "From the very beginning God decided that those who came to him—and all along he knew who would—should become like his Son, so that his Son would be the First, with many brothers" (TLB).

God's goal is that we become like His Son, meaning when He created us, He put the potential in us to become like Jesus. But that potential has to be released.

One of God's favorite tools to release that potential is change. Think about all the change He puts a tree through. Its journey begins as an acorn on a branch high above any adversity. But one day the branch releases the acorn, and it takes a long hard fall. Once it's on the ground, it's shoved, kicked, and trampled on until it's pushed below the soil.

Now in a dark and lonely place, it begins to sprout new life. It pushes through to the surface, only to enter a long season where all it can do is wait. Eventually, after enduring summer, fall, winter, and spring again and again—until the tree is tall enough to produce its own acorns—it finally reaches its full potential.

The adaptability of the tree is what enables its growth. It's not the tree's job to control the seasons. Its only job is to simply trust that every change is bringing it closer to its full potential.

If you're going to reach your full potential, you must carry the same outlook. In good seasons, know that God is working. In free-fall seasons, know that God is working. In dark lonely seasons, know that God is working. In seasons when you're pushing through, know that God is working. In waiting seasons, know that God is working. And in seasons when He asks you to give so others can benefit, know that He's still working.

In God's kingdom, longevity comes through adaptability.

When I look at where my life is currently, it's clear that God didn't need my *ability*; He wanted my *flexibility*. As a volunteer, I was flexible enough to become an intern. As an intern, I was flexible enough to become an assistant. As an assistant, I was flexible enough to take on a college ministry. As a college pastor, I was flexible enough to become an administrative pastor. As an administrative pastor, I was flexible enough to become a lead pastor. And as a lead pastor, I was flexible enough to become an author.

Turns out, in God's kingdom, longevity comes through adaptability.

2. Flexibility is necessary to stay spiritually full.

Spiritual adaptability doesn't come naturally; it comes only from letting God do a deep work in our hearts. Jesus taught on this specifically when a group of John the Baptist's disciples came to Him and asked why His disciples weren't practicing the dietary rules John adopted (Luke 5:33). In essence, they were used to things being done one way, and they were asking, "Why the change?"

Jesus responded with an illustration found in Luke 5:37–38: "No one pours new wine into old wineskins. Otherwise, the new wine will burst the skins; the wine will run out and the wineskins will be ruined. No, new wine must be poured into new wineskins."

What was clear for the first-century audience is unclear for us, so allow me to explain. Wineskins were containers made of sheepskin. When initially formed, they were soft and flexible. This made them able to accept a pour of new wine, because as the gasses from the fermentation expanded, the container expanded. The problem was when the once-pliable sheepskin became dry, hard, and brittle due to the Middle Eastern climate. If you poured new wine into an old container, it wouldn't expand. It would burst, making it unable to carry what was poured.

Jesus used this common item to explain how we relate to what God is doing on earth. The wine represents a fresh move of God's Spirit, and the container represents us. When we resist change, we eventually become dry. I know businesses that are dry and declining because they won't change. I know churches that are dry and dying because they won't change. I know people whose faith is dry—lacking fresh vision and joy—because they won't change.

Like the wineskin, when we're inflexible, we're unable to fulfill our purpose.

When a wineskin became hard, the owner had only two options: throw it away or put it through a renewal process where it was emptied, washed out, and massaged with oil. As the owner worked this process, the wineskin's pliability returned and it could receive a new pour. Like those containers, our hearts must go through a renewal process. One where every day we empty ourselves of our expectations or agendas and humbly ask the Holy Spirit to anoint us for what's ahead.

Here's the best news: God is ready to pour the moment you're renewed! He's ready to pour fresh ideas for a career relaunch, fresh attitudes between family members, fresh energy to people who've been worn down, and to some, fresh power to overcome spiritual opposition. All He's waiting for is for you to pray, *Whatever it looks like, whatever it sounds like, whatever You want it to be, I just need a fresh pouring of Your Spirit!*

As wonderful as this sounds, the sad news is that few ever receive this fresh pouring. In Luke 5:39, Jesus finished His comments by saying, "No one after drinking old wine wants the new, for they say, 'The old is better.'" He was saying that most people won't change because it takes intentional work, sacrifice, and courage. It's easier to stay with the old than go through the process to be renewed.

If you're tempted to keep fighting change, just know there's a cost—you'll miss the pour! Just because we say "The old is better" doesn't mean God stops pouring. It means He finds other places to pour.

In 1975, when Kodak owned the film development world, one of their engineers came to the board of directors claiming he'd invented the first digital camera. The board reviewed his findings and said, "No one would want to look at pictures on a screen," then passed on the project. Today Eastman Kodak is a different company because of that choice. The world was ready for something fresh, but Kodak refused to change.[1]

Where in your life is God trying to pour something fresh but can't because you won't change?

3. Flexibility is necessary to follow God's plan.

I want to close this chapter by acknowledging that sometimes the change we need is another church. Although I've explained how the power of staying planted can enhance your life, I realize sometimes God redirects us from one place to another.

Over the years I've noticed those transitions are some of the toughest. When you've poured your heart and soul into a faith community, leaving can feel like the death of a loved one. I've also seen people who were sincerely following God leave poorly. This not only damaged the place they were exiting but affected their ability to connect at the destination that followed.

How to Leave Well

I've come to believe how you leave one season dramatically affects how you enter the next. Therefore, I want to coach you on processing a local church transition.

First, take the motive test. This is where you get to the bottom of why you feel it's time to transition. We can have many motives for leaving a church, but not all of them are healthy. For this reason, I'm listing three motives that can be unhealthy and the appropriate response to them.

- If the motive is due to a *conflict*, then the appropriate response is to resolve it. You can attend a new church, but your heart won't be new. You'll still be struggling with the effects of offense, and that will hamper you from fully engaging. Resolve the conflict, and there may be no reason to leave—or at least you'll have peace as you go.

- If the motive is *confusion*, then the appropriate response is to have a conversation. Maybe there's been a change in a method or a leader, and you feel uncertain about the future. That's a reasonable feeling, but it's not a reason for leaving. Take time to sit with someone who will hear your concerns and provide clarity.

- If the motive is a *lack of confidence*, then the appropriate response is prayer. If you've lost confidence in your leader or local church's direction, take time to pray. You don't want to exit if the Holy Spirit wants to use you to strengthen a leader or be part of a solution. Set a reasonable timetable and commit to seeking God in prayer. You'll never regret giving God space to speak to you.

Then test God's will. If the motive is that you feel unsettled, then the appropriate response is to test God's will by applying the wisdom Jesus shared in Luke 13:

> A man planted a fig tree in his garden and came again and again to see if there was any fruit on it, but he was always disappointed. Finally, he said to his gardener, "I've waited three years, and there hasn't been a single fig! Cut it down. It's just taking up space in the garden." The gardener answered, "Sir, give it one more chance. Leave it another year, and I'll give it special attention and plenty of fertilizer. If we get figs next year, fine. If not, then you can cut it down."
>
> Luke 13:6–9 NLT

Like the man in Jesus' story, your unsettled feeling about your role in your current church can be summarized in these questions: Cut it off or continue to let it grow? Search for somewhere new or stay where you are?

If you find yourself in that unsettled space:

First, set a *reasonable timetable to make a decision*. The gardener said to give it another year, and this is good advice because situations or people rarely change overnight. Every timetable is different, but create a space for things to progress.

Second, *reinvest your best*. The gardener said, "I'll give it special attention. I'm going to dig in." Don't sit back with your arms crossed waiting for something to go wrong. Dig in and give your absolute best. Serve, give, pray, worship, encourage leaders. To live with peace for the future, you have to make sure you do everything possible to make it all work in the present.

Finally, *recognize God is growing you.* God is the gardener of your life, and He's able to increase your faith no matter where you are. Don't be surprised if part of this process includes a "fertilizer" season that's unpleasant. It isn't uncommon for there to be a period when you give your best but see little fruit. Even though that period stinks, trust that God is growing your character and will reward your effort.

Change for the Better

At the end of these steps, peace will mark the path you should take. If that path is leaving your current church, then do so with integrity. Talk to your leaders, thank them for their investment, ask for their blessing, and refuse to say anything that could damage a reputation.

Also, resist the urge to recruit or influence others. If asked, encourage them to adopt the process you used to clearly discover God's plan for them. Last, approach your search for a new faith community with the right mindset. Remember, you aren't shopping for comfort; you're asking God for your next assignment.

No matter the season you find yourself in, you can be sure that God has mapped out your life. Yes, it's filled with turns, dips, and climbs you didn't expect. But that's why it's essential that you decide what's more valuable—being in control or being flexible enough to follow. Control will leave you dry, but being adaptable will leave you in awe of all God can do.

We like the familiar because it's predictable. But God likes flexibility because it requires faith, and faith is what allows Him to move us forward.

> *Heavenly Father, I never want to miss out on what You're pouring out. Therefore, show me where I'm valuing my preferences over Yours. Help my will become pliable again, and stretch my faith so I can receive all You have for me. Amen.*

16

Commit to Unity

Being the parents of five young children is wonderful, but it also means Kayla and I have a front-row seat to unending conflict. Over the years, we've tried every type of incentive and disincentive, but we always seem to come up short. I expect Democrats and Republicans to find a path to peace before the hostility in our home ends!

In one season of desperation, we instituted the "everyone loses" rule, which basically says if anyone does anything to someone else, everyone is punished. If one complains about the TV, everyone loses TV. If one takes another's snack, everyone loses their snack. This no-nonsense rule was necessary because my kids were content to keep fighting. But as their father, I was willing to take whatever steps necessary to end the strife.

You may be surprised to know that our heavenly Father has a similar desire. For Him, unity is a top priority.

In Psalm 133:1, we discover that God considers it good and pleasing for us to dwell in unity. And in verse 3 we read, "For there the Lord has given the gift of life that lasts forever" (NLV).

When we give attention to unity, God gives us a gift or unique blessing. But if something can be given, then something can also be taken. This means when we lose the practice of unity, we also lose the blessing of God.

We tend to think God rewards the spiritual activities we do. But in God's kingdom, spiritual practices aren't more powerful than petty divisions. This means you can't out-sing being hateful toward your spouse. You can't out-pray the prejudice in your heart. And your devotions don't work if you dishonor leaders. The hard truth is God commands blessing on unity and witholds blessing from division—no matter how spiritual we appear!

> *In God's kingdom, spiritual practices aren't more powerful than petty divisions.*

There's no better picture of this than in a story found in Genesis.

Lessons from Babel

After surviving the flood, Noah and his family started repopulating the earth. Generation after generation was born, people migrated, and the first significant city was built while everyone in the world still spoke a common language.

Then God spotted a problem . . . and responded:

> As people moved eastward, they found a plain in Shinar and settled there. They said to each other, "Come, let's make bricks and bake them thoroughly." They used brick instead of stone, and tar for mortar. Then they said, "Come, let us build ourselves a city, with a tower that reaches to the heavens, so that we may make a name for ourselves; otherwise, we will be scattered over the face of the whole earth." But the LORD came down to see the city and the tower the people were building. The LORD said, "If as one people speaking the same language they have begun to do this, then nothing they plan to do will be impossible for them. Come, let us go down and confuse their language so they will not understand each other." So

the LORD scattered them from there over all the earth, and they stopped building the city. That is why it was called Babel—because there the LORD confused the language of the whole world.

Genesis 11:2–9

What a sight it must have been to see an entire group of people in partnership on this project. But though their goal was clear, their hearts weren't set on honoring God. Their motive was to display the greatness of humanity's ingenuity. Nonetheless, what was happening in Babel is a reminder that unity is powerful and even works for those with the wrong motives.

The lesson of this account is that mankind's definition of unity and God's definition are quite different. You may have noticed a detail early in the passage—that the entire project was built with brick, not stone. In Scripture, no detail is without meaning, and one of the great things about the Bible is that it interprets itself. Meaning, if snakes are dangerous in Genesis, their mention implies something dangerous in Revelation. So the idea of exchanging stone for bricks carries meaning.

Throughout Scripture, mankind always uses bricks in prideful displays. For example, bricks were used in Babel's tower, in Egypt's oppression of the Hebrews, and in Jericho's walls. Each is an example of humans opposing God. But God always uses stones for kingdom displays. Stones were stacked to commemorate entering the promised land, and stone was used for the temple that housed God's presence. Additionally, 1 Peter 2:5 says, "You also are like living stones. As you come to Christ, you are being built into a house for worship" (NIRV).

These details teach us that when it comes to unity, bricks and stones represent two different mindsets.

Bricks are pressed, but stones are placed.

Too many people today approach relationships with a preconceived mold they force others into. All their friends' interests have to be the same as theirs. They'll respect someone only if their views are the same as theirs, and some even question another's faith if their practices aren't the same as theirs. In essence they're saying, "Unless you press yourself into the mold of my expectations, I can't accept you."

But while we try to press people into molds, God accepts each person as a masterpiece. He saw value in us before we saw it in ourselves. He didn't force us to change before accepting us. He accepted us as we were and placed us in His kingdom. He made you and me a son or daughter before we looked anything like Him!

If you have a brick mentality, listen up! Your job isn't to change everyone; it's to love everyone. You do the loving, and the Holy Spirit will do the changing. If you can't accept someone because of their sin, then you have more faith in sin than you have in the work of Christ. Call me naïve if you wish, but I believe if I love someone and constantly point them toward Jesus, He has the power to break their every struggle, free them from sin, and reframe what they see.

Bricks are about uniformity, but stones are appreciated for their uniqueness.

Brick thinking says we have to talk alike, look alike, vote alike, and think alike to achieve unity. But true unity requires diversity. For example, God's definition of marriage is one man and one woman joined together, thus becoming one, not becoming the same. A marriage is diversity in unity!

Kayla and I are very different, but we are one. We're diverse, but we share a common goal. Now, I'll confess that at the beginning of our marriage, I was a brick head! I wanted Kayla to be naturally task oriented, scheduled, and strategic—like me. But my wife isn't any of those things naturally, and as long as I thought like a brick, we had issues. I stayed frustrated, and she was often hurt thinking I disliked who she was.

Then one day I was in prayer when the Holy Spirit opened my eyes to the reality that if God already had one of me in this marriage, we didn't need another. What Kayla possessed is what we needed. What *I* needed. I needed her spontaneity, tenderness, and grace. That shift in thinking was freeing and allowed me to fully appreciate who she is!

Listen, you're great, but one of you is enough! If you want to enjoy life, you need the uniqueness that comes from others. Uniformity will make you *comfortable*, but it won't make you *better*. Only when you allow different gifts or views and appreciate people for who God made them to be will you become who God intended *you* to be. Remember, unity doesn't tolerate diversity; it celebrates it!

Bricks are what the enemy uses to divide. The name *devil* in the original Greek language of the New Testament is *diablos*, and the root word is divider. From the core of his being, the enemy hates unity because he hates God (who is the picture of perfect unity as the Father, Son, and Spirit working as one). He knows that if he can cause division, it will break the unity, and a lack of unity will keep God's blessing away. This is why some New Testament letters instruct churches to put out those who cause division. It implies that if you want God's blessing, you can't keep divisive people around.

When you tolerate division, you welcome the enemy's plan into your life. And you can always tell if you're allowing him to frame your thinking by how you treat others. If you treat people like common bricks instead of God-shaped stones, the enemy has you blinded.

In his book *Man's Search for Meaning*, Viktor Frankl documented his experiences as a Holocaust victim. He was loaded onto an overcrowded railroad car with other Jewish prisoners, and when he arrived at his camp, he was stripped of his clothing, photos, personal belongings, and any distinguishing features. Next, the Nazis took away every prisoner's name and gave them numbers. Viktor's number was 119,104. From that day forward, he wasn't a man but a number. And that step allowed the guards to carry out the atrocities we've all heard about.[1] This illustrates that once you *dehumanize*, it becomes easy to *demonize* (or advance the devil's cause).

I'm afraid that's what some of us do daily. And my prayer is that this chapter wakes us up to the fact that they're not just a coworker; they're a child of God. They're not just an aimless young adult or irrelevant senior; they're the apple of God's eye. They're not just a bad driver or slow waitress; they're fearfully and wonderfully made by God. They're not just police officers or protesters; they're the reason Jesus allowed Himself to be hung on a cross and poured out His life.

Never forget that the enemy uses bricks to divide, but Jesus rolled away a stone to ensure that no creed, color, or culture misses His extravagant love!

This is why the apostle Paul wrote the Ephesian church saying, "Make every effort to keep the unity of the Spirit through the bond of peace" (Ephesians 4:3). Paul's language is emphatic, and it communicates that we should go to whatever length necessary to stay unified.

How Do We Keep Unity?

Though the question of how we keep unity could be answered several ways, I remind you what God addressed at Babel—the people's tongues. If you and I truly want to stay unified and receive the blessing of God, then three things are required of us.

First, own up to any division in your heart. The first step to unity is not God changing "them." It's God changing me. Every person reading this book has an inherited view to be reframed, an attitude to be reformed, or an offense to be reconciled. The question is whether we'll admit it and submit it to God's will. Will we act according to God's standard and not our own reasoning? Everyone has a reason to be offended, but the hard truth is if you keep the offense, then you want your feelings more than you want the blessing of God.

Second, shut up when your words are doing damage. Maybe we're more divided than ever because social media has given us a platform to fight on every front. I'll be the first to admit that it's tempting to engage someone who's misrepresenting a subject or attacking something I care about. But I've learned it's best to just keep scrolling. Algorithms and online audiences never reward measured responses. The internet is built for extremes. Therefore, determine to not engage every goofy comment. Those folks have been crazy for a long time, and your reply won't fix them!

Unfortunately, too many Christians are combative and want to be right more than they want to restore unity. But this approach is in direct opposition to Paul's instructions in 2 Timothy 2:23–25 (NLT):

> Don't get involved in foolish, ignorant arguments that only start fights. A servant of the Lord must not quarrel but must be kind to everyone, be able to teach, and be patient with difficult people. Gently instruct those who oppose the truth. Perhaps God will change those people's hearts, and they will learn the truth.

Whether you're interacting with an unbeliever or a believer, you're called to be a "peacemaker" (Matthew 5:9). Notice you're called to *make* peace, not *find* peace. This means you have a responsibility to create peace.

Professor and author J. S. Knox said, "You cannot antagonize and influence at the same time."[2] This means before you express yourself, you must ensure that you've allowed the Word of God to frame your view and the Spirit of God to frame your response. Culture has a "truth," politicians have a "truth," and we have our own "truth," but only God's truth and Spirit bring life.

Don't be confused. Unity doesn't mean we always agree. Unity doesn't mean you can't have an opinion. But unity does value the blessing of the Lord over putting someone in their place. Sharing my opinion is not worth losing my peace.

Finally, speak up. Once your heart is clean and you have God's mindset, God will use your mouth to encourage, bless, include, heal, and much more.

Sometime ago I was in Hawaii vacationing with my family. I had just sat down by the pool preparing to dive into a book when I recognized the guy sitting beside me. It was Miles McPherson, who after playing four seasons in the NFL planted a church in San Diego, California.

After I introduced myself, Miles and I talked about family, life, and ministry. As our time came to an end, I thanked him for a book he authored titled *The Third Option*. It's a book on racial reconciliation that helped our team lead our church in the wake of nationwide protests on race relations.

In that book Miles shares about attending an event to hear an acquaintance speak. In the beginning of the session, the speaker, who was Black, made several humorous comments that had the audience laughing. Then to Miles's surprise, the speaker pointed to him and made fun of him for being "almost Black." Although the speaker received a big laugh from the crowd, Miles recounted how much the remark wounded him. In the weeks that followed, Miles noticed his heart growing harder toward this person. When their name came up, he felt resistance toward honoring them, and when left alone with his thoughts, he felt anger and resentment growing.

This was a critical juncture for Miles—he had to decide to continue avoiding the situation, exacerbating the issue, or address it head-on. Miles prayed about the situation and decided to initiate a conversation.

With the Holy Spirit's help, Miles approached the conversation without dishonoring the person who hurt him. He clearly expressed how the comment had caused him pain and then patiently listened. Turns out, the speaker meant no harm but understood the damage caused. The person apologized to Miles, and Miles freely forgave. Though I'm sure this conversation was uncomfortable, the results speak for themselves: unity was restored and both parties enjoyed peace.[3]

Unity isn't a byproduct of ignoring issues; it's the byproduct of identifying issues and being brave enough to handle them in a godly way. When you see someone treated poorly, are you brave enough to speak up? When you're offended, are you brave enough to sit down with the person who hurt you? If something you've done caused someone else pain, are you brave enough to apologize? Speaking up, not sweeping things under the rug, is how sin is stopped and unity is restored.

Unity is the byproduct of identifying issues and being brave enough to handle them in a godly way.

Though the steps necessary to maintain unity can be uncomfortable, remember that the reward is uncommon. This is best displayed when you compare what happened in Babel to what happened at the birth of the church in Acts 2:

> When the Day of Pentecost had fully come, they were all with one accord in one place. And suddenly there came a sound from heaven, as of a rushing mighty wind, and it filled the whole house where they were sitting. Then there appeared to them divided tongues, as of fire, and one sat upon each of them. And they were all filled with the Holy Spirit and began to speak with other tongues, as the Spirit gave them utterance.
>
> Acts 2:1–4 NKJV

The only difference in the unity displayed at Babel and the unity displayed in the upper room was who was in charge. At Babel, the people wanted their way. In the upper room, those praying wanted God's way. This passage is a reminder that when our hearts are submitted to God, the result is a move of God. If you read Acts 2 in its entirety, you'll see the uncommon blessing unity brings:

It makes you stronger. Their unified hearts gave God the green light to send the Holy Spirit. It was the single greatest interaction any human had ever had with God. The Spirit didn't visit them; it indwelled them. People who'd been denying Jesus and hiding from religious authorities were filled with the Holy Spirit, transformed, and began living a supernatural life.

It causes you to stand out. As they poured out of the house and into the city, people immediately took notice and wanted what they had. Today, division is so common, but when a diverse group of people submit their opinions, preferences, politics, and passions to unify around a single purpose (Jesus), the world takes notice.

It allows you to see God's glory. The Holy Spirit empowered them, and then the most unifying moment in human history took place:

> At that time there were devout Jews from every nation living in Jerusalem. When they heard the loud noise, everyone came running, and they were bewildered to hear their own languages being spoken by the believers. They were completely amazed. "How can this be?" they exclaimed. "These people are all from Galilee, and yet we hear them speaking in our own native languages!"
>
> Acts 2:5–8 NLT

In Genesis 11, God divided the language of the people because they were unified around pride. In Acts 2, God unified the language of the people of God, and the result—for they were telling about God's wonderful works (verse 11)—was a revival that swept the world. Two thousand years later, we're still experiencing its results.

Do you want to see a move of God in your home, workplace, church, or city? Then determine that you'll live a life committed to unity. Not in theory, but in practice every day. The greatest displays of God's glory happen when God's people display unity.

God, please recalibrate my mind to value unity, like You do. Help me see and celebrate the uniqueness You've placed in each person. And set a guard over my mouth so that my words preserve peace in my home, workplace, and church. In Jesus' name, amen.

17

Reach Out in Love

During the summer of 1859, a French acrobat known as Blondin stunned the world by walking on a tightrope 160 feet above Niagara Falls. According to those present:

> After pushing a wheelbarrow across [the falls] while blindfolded . . . he asked his audience, "Do you believe I can carry a person across in this wheelbarrow?" Of course the crowd shouted that yes, they believed! It was then that Blondin posed the question—"Who will get in the wheelbarrow?" Of course . . . none did.[1]

When it comes to love, I think too often the church is guilty of acting like Blondin's crowd. We cheer for feats of love. We applaud when we see others love. We scream for others to walk in love. But when we're invited to step out and love ourselves, we go silent hoping someone else will volunteer.

Even a casual reading of Scripture gives the impression that nothing is more important to God than love. In 1 Peter 4:8 we're instructed, "Above all, love each other deeply." In 1 Corinthians 16:14 we're told to "do everything in love." And in 1 John 4:8 we're confronted with the fact that "whoever does not love does not know God, because God is love."

The unfortunate truth is that God's highest priority is often hard to find among His people. After all, isn't that why church hurt exists? Although many types of church hurt occur, they're all derived from the same place—a lack of love.

A Loveless Church

So how is it that the people who've been loved the most often love the least? How is Jesus' most important message too often the one missing from the movement He founded? I don't have all the answers, but I do think a portion of the problem lies in the following:

First, we think love is a lesson we've already learned. Sometime ago, I was driving when out of nowhere I sensed the Holy Spirit say, *I'm going to teach you to love.* I wasn't thinking about love, I wasn't singing about love, and to be honest, the statement hit me as a little odd. Because frankly, I thought I already knew how to love. After all, I have a wife, my love for her has resulted in five kids, and I love those five kids fiercely. I also pastor a church, and by nature a pastor is someone who loves people.

So when it came to love, I felt like I already knew more than the average person. The fact that the Holy Spirit said He was going to teach me to love seemed unnecessary—until someone cut me off in traffic a few moments later. Without any hesitation, I followed closely and gave them a death stare! That's when I heard it again: I'm going to teach you to love. Suddenly, the statement made more sense. Turns out I still needed higher learning when it came to love.

I've also discovered that most of what we know about love has been informed more by culture than by Jesus Christ, and that's why we have such a misunderstanding about it:

Culture portrays love as something that happens by chance. People say things like, "We just fell in love," as if love were a hole they stumbled into. But Jesus teaches that love is a choice we make again and again despite someone else's attitude or actions.

Culture describes love as an emotion. But Jesus makes it clear that love is not love until it acts. This is why Romans 5:8 says God demonstrates His love for us. Jesus didn't limit His love to how He felt; He displayed it by carrying a cross.

Culture suggests love is too often temporary. Have you ever heard someone say, "We're no longer in love"? But 1 Corinthians 13:7 tells us love "perseveres," meaning it pushes past temporary feelings and remains through every season.

Finally, culture presents love as optional, meaning it's selective. It prefers those who treat it well and rejects those who do not. Though this idea is commonly accepted, it's not endorsed by Christ. According to Jesus, love is the Great Commandment—to love everyone the same way we love God.

Looking at these differences makes two things clear. First, our standard of love is very different from Jesus' standard. Second, many of the people who fill the seats of churches, sing worship songs, and listen to sermons are missing the mark when it comes to fulfilling their mission.

Our Love Tends to Retract as Life Goes On

No one sets out to become less loving, but it's undeniable that over time our love pulls back. For example, children generally love everybody. My kids will engage with anyone, talk to anyone, and hug anyone. But something happens as we age—that childlike love begins to shrink back.

We recoil from loving all, to loving some, to loving a select few. The list of the people we love grows shorter, and the list of the people we loathe grows longer. And without realizing it, we can pull back so much that our love includes only people who look like us, sound like us, vote like us, agree with us, or believe like us.

There's a danger in not acknowledging this tendency—we begin to live according to our definition of love instead of God's! You see,

God defined His love in John 3:16: "God so loved the world that he gave his one and only Son, that whoever believes in him shall not perish but have eternal life." God's love is so inclusive that it includes the whole world. Our love is a "select people at select times" type of love, but God's is an "all people, all the time" type of love. When we narrow God's definition of love, we negate the very purpose of the body of Christ on earth.

When we narrow God's definition of love, we negate the very purpose of the body of Christ on earth.

And as my sister-in-law Amber discovered, this can happen anywhere. After graduating high school, Amber followed her dream of leveraging her life to help others. Inspired by missionaries and others who ministered to the most marginalized, she began attending a ministry school in hopes of being on the front lines of what God was doing for those struggling. Though the school's rigid authoritarian approach and priority to preserve their list of rules rubbed her the wrong way, she persevered.

In her third year Amber and a group of fellow students were assigned to help facilitate a program that provided tutoring and activities for the children of single mothers who'd escaped homelessness or an abusive situation. Some of the families were there by choice, and some were there by court order. Though Amber was barely an adult herself, she took this assignment seriously, realizing she may be one of the few people who'd ever shown these kids love.

One evening she was tasked with overseeing a group of elementary-aged boys as they played basketball. One of them had been around for a few months as part of a court order, and Amber had noticed that he often had pronounced bruises on his arms, neck, and face. When she asked about them, he'd always say he'd fallen. He also had a history of aggressive behavior toward other kids. These things made Amber concerned that something was wrong at home.

When the basketball time concluded, he was the last to be picked up as his mother was coming from a class herself. When she arrived, she asked about his behavior. Amber told her he'd had a good day except for a scuffle with another boy.

The mother was clearly upset as she gave her son a stern look and led him out the door. Concerned that she was disproportionately distressed, Amber followed and came upon the woman repeatedly banging her son against the cinder block wall while yelling at him about his behavior.

Amber ran to get help, and some staff separated the child from his mother. The boy's head was cut, and he was bawling. Amber was whisked away to another building by a staff member to ensure she'd not been hurt.

After her exam, Amber asked the staff member if they'd called Child Protective Services, and she was simply told, "The boy is being cared for." Something didn't sit right with her, but she trusted the staff member.

The next day she was called to the program director's office. Nervous as this director was known for being strong—even militaristic—Amber took a seat and recounted what happened. The director listened and then assured her the situation was being handled.

When Amber raised the idea of Child Protective Services, the director quickly dismissed the idea, making it clear that they should refrain from further involvement and instead trust the Holy Spirit to work in the mother's heart. Amber couldn't believe what she heard, and she felt helpless. She'd notified those over her, but they'd chosen to do nothing.

Though the director's position that day was to pull back, Amber refuses to allow that to be the story of how she loves. Today, she's a licensed social worker whose responsibilities regularly include ensuring children escape abusive situations. Though she wasn't in a position to help that young boy at basketball camp, she's spent the rest of her life reaching out to ensure others like him are cared for.

The frustration Amber felt is a frustration many people have with the church today. They see too many believers pulling back from loving the world God loves the way He expects them to. They've even pulled back from loving each other, preferring to stay uninvolved in anything that looks like it could be messy.

Jesus' Love Always Reaches Out

As I observe the unrest in our culture, I can't help but wonder if the world is so broken because we're leaving love in the pews. Instead of showing affection, we argue. Instead of giving a piece of our heart, we give a piece of our minds. Instead of extending a hand, we keep people at arm's length. Little by little, limit by limit, we've made God's inclusive love into an exclusive love. And our loss of love is why we, the church, have lost so much influence.

If we will just get back to caring over condemning, mending people over crafting another post, and loving over lecturing, our buildings wouldn't be able to contain the people who'll want to be there. Christlike love is compelling, contagious, and exactly what people are searching for!

This was a lesson Jesus prioritized when teaching His own disciples through ministry: "Large crowds followed Jesus as he came down the mountainside. Suddenly, a man with leprosy approached him and knelt before him. 'Lord,' the man said, 'if you are willing, you can heal me and make me clean'" (Matthew 8:1–2 NLT).

The man in this story had leprosy. In the first century, that meant he was untouchable, considered unclean, and disregarded in a way that's hard for us to grasp. In a physical sense, his body was deteriorating. The discolored patches and open sores would have left his face unrecognizable. The stench from rotting flesh would have been intolerable. But leprosy wasn't just a physical disease; it carried a spiritual statement. It was assumed a leper was cursed by God. That's why the leper said to Jesus, "If you are willing, you can heal me and make me clean." The leper knew Jesus had the ability, but he doubted Jesus' desire.

You can imagine how the large crowd following Jesus would have split trying to avoid this man. Parents would have pulled their children back, and bystanders would have looked opposite his direction.

Now, Mark's account of this story has an added detail: "A man with leprosy came to him and begged him on his knees, 'If you are willing, you can make me clean.' Jesus was indignant" (Mark 1:40–41).

Why does Mark note Jesus' anger? Remember, Matthew 8 comes after Matthew 5, 6, and 7, known as the Sermon on the Mount. Jesus' most famous teaching includes strong themes, such as loving the poor, loving your enemy, and reaching out to the most broken in spirit. So as Jesus watched this crowd pull back, anger welled up in Him. They had just listened to the greatest sermon on love, and yet they were pulling back from someone who needed it!

In His frustration, Jesus decides not to reteach the sermon but to demonstrate it in what must have been a jaw-dropping act: "He reached out his hand and touched the man. 'I am willing,' he said. 'Be clean!' Immediately the leprosy left him and he was cleansed" (Mark 1:41–42).

Three Characteristics of Christlike Love

The cycle of church hurt has to end, and the church must regain its authority. But those are both possible only if you and I live reaching out in love. If you're up for that challenge and want to be part of the solution in your part of the world, then strive to embody the following three characteristics when it comes to love:

1. Seeing the overlooked

One day Sawyer and I were talking about superheroes when he asked, "Dad, what superpower would you like?" My initial thought was the power to remove calories from ice cream. But I knew Sawyer wouldn't understand that, so I asked him the same question. He chose the power to turn invisible so he could sneak into the freezer to get ice cream. Like father like son!

Here's what you and I know that Sawyer has yet to learn: being invisible isn't a superpower; it's a struggle.

214

The physical pain of leprosy was unbearable, but it didn't compare to the pain of being invisible. The pain of being avoided. The pain of being ignored.

In the four Gospels, over and over we read, "Jesus saw." Seeing was the launching point for how He transformed lives. To love means to see what Jesus would see and act as He would act. Most often, we don't see the miracles we want to see because of the way we see. Our eyes are conditioned by schedules, tasks, and the pull of life to the point that we see problems, not people. We see inconvenience, not individuals. We see obstacles to our agenda, not objects of God's love. Until we open our eyes to the needs around us, God won't use us to meet those needs in supernatural ways.

Jesus saw a man with leprosy everyone else had learned to ignore. Why? Because He didn't mind being interrupted. He wasn't so busy, so self-absorbed, that He couldn't see someone who needed to be loved. If I want God to use me, I must get used to being interrupted. Loving like Jesus means I'm open enough to allow God to interrupt me.

What we call ministry and what Jesus called ministry are too often different. We say ministry is holding a high-profile position, presenting or performing on a stage, or bearing a title. But Jesus didn't need any of that to serve. Scripture says He did it "as He went along" (John 9:1). And the main place you do the work of God is as *you* go along.

Look for defeated people and help them start over. Look for grieving people and be there for them. Look for lonely people and become their friend. Look for angry people and show them kindness. Reaching out begins with seeing the overlooked and saying to them, "I see you!"

2. Listening to those who need to be heard

Jesus didn't just see this man; He also listened to him. Love always includes listening. But let's be honest, listening is tough to do. We've got places to be, distractions abound, and no one enjoys hearing about all the bad in someone's life.

Sometime ago, a friend introduced me to someone they knew. Now, I'm going to let you in on a secret: people can get, well, weird around pastors. Some worry that I know or will guess all their dark secrets, some want to debate theological issues, and some see being with me as an opportunity to unpack their whole life story.

This guy was the latter. He gave me a personal tour through every decade of his life, and just about the time I thought he was winding down, he took a rabbit trail off memory lane. On the outside I was smiling, but on the inside I was praying someone would pull a fire alarm.

He finally came to a close, and just as I was about to sprint away, I felt the Holy Spirit nudge me to ask him a question. Immediately, I thought, *No way! If I do, he'll start up again.* But that's when I heard the Holy Spirit say once more, *I'm going to teach you how to love.* So I asked a question, and the man's eyes lit up because someone had shown interest in his story.

I've learned listening says a lot. "Huh?" you say. "Listening means I'm not saying anything." But when you listen you show someone you care, and that opens their heart to believing God cares.

Researcher Joe Aldridge tells us that after being a Christian for two years, the average follower of Jesus no longer has a single significant relationship with a non-believer.[2] So before we fret about what to say, let's focus on the fact that we need to get close to people who are far from God. Do you know the best way to build a relationship? Become a great listener.

3. Touching the untouchable

I can hear you thinking, *Joe, I'm with you up to this point. I'll do better at seeing and listening. But I'm drawing the line at touching people.* I get it; I've never been a touchy-feely person. I'm sure I've got hand sanitizer in every drawer of my desk. And if I'd been one of Jesus' disciples that day, I probably would have fainted as I watched Him touch the decaying, infected, and contagious hand of a leper.

But beyond fearing contagion, why would I have that reaction? The same reason all religious people tend to pull back from infected people—we have more confidence in what's wrong than in the One who makes things right!

The Bible says the man was healed "immediately," reminding us that there's something more contagious than leprosy—love. People can doubt sermons, but they can't doubt love. People can argue with doctrine, but they can't argue with love. They can turn away from programs, but they'll turn to love. After love they'll never be the same. Love pushes out fear. Love drowns their guilt. Love removes their shame. Love opens their heart. Love turns what they thought they knew about God upside down. Love is the most powerful force on earth, and it never fails!

As we conclude this chapter, I must point out the fact that throughout the four Gospels we see multiple accounts of Jesus healing people without touching them. He simply spoke and healing occurred. But on this day, He chose to touch this leper. I think that was because He wanted to do more than heal the man's body. He wanted to heal his soul from all the rejection, loneliness, and shame he'd endured over the years.

If influence is your goal, then love is a necessity. But it will require you to roll up your sleeves and get your hands "dirty."

Wheelbarrows of Love

Years ago, Kayla and I had a neighbor who was nice but also a bit difficult. He was one of those guys who kept a perfect yard and had no problem pointing out the flaws in mine. He was in his seventies and retired, and as soon as he discovered I was a pastor, he was sure to let me know he wanted nothing to do with church. He'd grown up in a strict religious environment and had spent his adult life avoiding anything labeled Christian. Anytime I'd get anywhere near the subject of church, he'd shut down the conversation.

One day I had a day off all to myself. Kayla and the kids were away, and there was nothing I had to do. I could watch TV, go to a movie, go to the gym—whatever I wanted.

I happened to look out the window and notice this neighbor had a huge load of mulch in his driveway, and he was moving it by wheelbarrow to the back of his house. I watched him take a load and thought, *Thank God that isn't me.* Then I immediately sensed the Holy Spirit say, *Go help him move the mulch.*

Sometimes I respond even to the Holy Spirit without thinking, and I said *You go help him. You can split seas, you can move mulch!* You can imagine how that went. So I gave in and spent the next two hours moving load after load. Finally, the last load was delivered, my neighbor thanked me, and I found the Icy Hot.

A month or so later, I heard a knock on our door. It was this neighbor, who sheepishly said, "My daughter is having surgery next week, and we're a little worried about it. I got to thinking, would you or your church mind praying for her?"

I smiled. *Thought you didn't want to talk about church!* But I said, "Of course we'll pray." We even sent flowers and a member of a care team to visit her, and I'm happy to say the surgery went well.

The day I spent moving mulch didn't result in my neighbor surrendering his life to Christ, but his heart did open a little more to the God I believe will change his life one day. Christians have the greatest message in the world, but we must earn the right to share it, and we earn it through reaching out in love.

God, as I read this chapter, it became clear that I need to relearn love according to Your standard. You have loved me so freely and deeply, and please help me channel that to those around me. Finally, please convict me every time my love retracts instead of reaching out. Amen.

Conclusion

From Mess to Masterpiece

Frank Lloyd Wright was a famed American architect whose many designs were so extraordinary that in the twentieth century they sparked an architectural movement that stretched around the globe. And when asked which of his designs was his favorite, he'd always say, "The next one."[1] He'd designed many structures, but his response was decisive. Something in him believed the best was yet to come.

Do you believe the best is yet to come for you? Your past has had painful moments so intense—probably with anger as well as sorrow—that you didn't think you'd survive. But you did! And now as your wounds begin to scar and you regain your strength little by little, my concern is that your heart will heal but your eyes of faith will remain dim. God's will isn't just for you to recover from your pain; He wants to redeem your pain for a purpose. But for that to happen, your attitude has to expect the best is yet to come.

The Truth about Your Attitude

Often in the wake of pain, we're so preoccupied with our feelings that we forget the power of our attitude. And to harness that power positively we must remember two important facts.

First, nothing is more consequential than your attitude. If you look up the word *attitude* in the dictionary, one definition refers to the orientation of an aircraft relative to the direction of travel. A pilot I know named Shane has explained to me that planes have a gauge known as the attitude indicator. It tells the pilot if the nose of the aircraft is pointed up or down. This is particularly helpful in situations with limited visibility. In good weather you can see the orientation of the aircraft, but in bad weather you often can't. So this gauge keeps you from trusting only your feelings, which could lead to a crash.

I like that analogy, because it's a reminder that more than any other factor, the orientation of your attitude determines if you soar or crash in life.

Second, your attitude is not the product of your circumstance. I know it's hard to believe, but the *American Journal of Medical Genetics* documents a remarkable study of a single group of people who report off-the-chart positivity: "Among those surveyed, 99% indicated that they were happy with their lives, 97% liked who they are, and 96% liked how they look. 99% expressed love for their family."[2] Who are these people? Individuals with Down syndrome. Despite their challenges, joy and contentment marks their outlook.

Your attitude can give you an advantage as you move forward, but the key to recapturing an expectant outlook is to believe that, despite feelings of despair and a lack of evidence around you, God loves you and is gathering the details of your situation to creatively craft something purposeful and beautiful. In short, you must believe God can turn your mess into a masterpiece!

A Perspective from Pottery

Years ago after a dinner date, Kayla and I casually strolled down a street that carried us past all sorts of specialty shops. At each storefront we looked in the window, taking in its unique items. Eventually, we stopped at a pottery studio that offered classes. I immediately imagined us reenacting that romantic scene from the classic movie *Ghost* where Patrick Swayze sits behind Demi Moore as she crafts a vase at her potter's wheel. (I pitched the idea, but Kayla didn't seem open to it.)

As we stood there looking over the space, I noticed the front of the store near the window was pristine and posh, displaying the resident artist's work. But a little farther back was the studio that housed big buckets of plaster, stacks of worn molds, and a wall of recently used aprons. This area was messy and where the real work took place. No class was in session that evening, but I could see someone back there working with a potter's wheel.

I couldn't help but remember that Scripture describes God as a potter (Jeremiah 18:6). I love that, because it reminds me He's chosen to both personally and intricately mold each of our lives.

As we turned to leave, my eyes spanned the entire space from the buckets of plaster to the finished products in the front, and I thought, *Most people probably never appreciate what messes those masterpieces once were.*

What's true for pottery is also true for people. When we see people who are whole, happy, and operating in their strengths, we never consider the mess they came from. And this limited perspective limits our faith for what God can do in our own lives. So I remind you that our worst moments are often what God uses to bring forth His best work.

I was recently captured by artist Phil Hansen's story. Pursuing his dream, he went to art school and developed a specialty called pointillism—a technique that uses small, distinct dots to form an image.

Then one day Phil noticed a small tremor in his hand. It worsened, and eventually he lost the ability to hold his hand steady. The harder he tried, the worse the shake became. In despair, Phil gave up on his dream, dropped out of art school, and left the art community entirely.

Years passed, and realizing he still wanted to be an artist, he saw a neurologist and discovered he had permanent nerve damage. But the doctor asked a question that struck a chord: "Why don't you just embrace the shake?" In essence, he was saying perhaps Phil could figure out how to incorporate his brokenness into a new way of producing art.

Phil began experimenting, letting his creativity flow, and the most incredible thing happened. The shake he thought destroyed his artistic ability redirected him to his most powerful work. Today Phil's art is world-renowned. He's won numerous awards, and his TED Talk on "Embracing the Shake" has inspired millions.[3]

The Process: From Agony to Art

Phil's story and so many others proclaim a clear message: God's specialty is transforming messes into masterpieces. He has a way of crafting our most agonizing seasons into art. But for that to happen, we have to recognize there's a crafting process before we're placed on display. Often, it's our lack of understanding this process that causes us to lose faith and give up. So allow me to lay out the four steps to God's redeeming process in hopes of helping you identify where you are.

1. Admit your expectations were shattered.

When we set out on the journey of life, we have in mind how the journey will go. From an early age we're taught to pursue our dreams and shape our reality, so we adopt the mold that takes us there. Typically, that's graduating from school. Falling in love. Seeing our career rise. Gaining influence. Having a family. Living out our purpose. Enjoying life.

Let me say there's nothing wrong with having a dream or charting a course—as long as we remember molds are breakable. If we've learned anything from the past, it's that life has breaking points that often shatter our expectations.

For some of you, the breaking point was when you learned about the affair. For others, it was when the addiction was made public. Or when the company downsized or ministry ended. Or when the doctor gave the diagnosis. Or when bankruptcy, a breakup, or a situation you wish was only a bad dream occurred.

Regardless of the details, I know that when the breaking occurred, you jumped into action. You didn't sit idly by; you began sweeping up the situation and picking up the pieces. That's because we were taught and believe that with enough determination and grit, we can glue things back together.

This may be where you are. You've dug deep and worked hard to hold your dream, home, or ministry together. But in the frenzy, you've misbelieved the next stage in the process is restoration when in reality it's usually a wearing down.

2. Realize time has ground at your hope.

This is where you were broken by the words "I don't love you," and then ground by two years of divorce proceedings. Or you were broken by the results of the scan, and then ground by three years of treatment. Or you were broken by the unexpected death, and then ground by unpredictable waves of grief. Or you were broken by the betrayal, and then ground by years of trying to find a new faith community you could trust.

We live in a broken world, and we're not surprised when things break. But what do you do when things aren't just broken but ground beyond repair? At least with broken, there's hope you can glue the pieces back together. But in the grinding of time, we lose hope, because we realize there's no going back to what once was. After all, you can't repair dust!

Hopelessness is a hard place to be. It turns our hearts cynical and our thoughts doubtful. It's the place where you're certain you can't fix your circumstance and assume God has moved on. This assumption is rooted in the idea that because God is holy, pure, and seated high atop a throne, He wants nothing to do with the mess your marriage, emotional state, or ministry is in.

As someone who's visited hopelessness more than once, I want you to know there's a problem with your assumption—namely, it's most likely based on secondhand information. Most people allow culture, their parents, or some random person on social media define who God is. But I think your faith is important enough to not depend on secondhand definitions. You must discover for yourself who God is, and if you do, I'm certain you'll also discover He's not some distant deity unwilling to enter our messy situations.

Sometimes we impose qualities on God that don't make sense.

When my daughter Remi was around three years old, she was outside playing, and after a few minutes she came to the door covered from head to toe in mud. We'd sent her out in a white cotton coat, but she returned in a dark shade of brown.

She was a mess, but do you know what I didn't say? I didn't say, "Remi, just stay outside! I'm so disappointed in you. Until you clean yourself up, you can't come in here." Of course I didn't say that, because I'm her father, and I know messes happen. When they do, it's my job to help her, not avoid her.

Know this: you have a heavenly Father who loves you more than I could ever love my kids. And if Scripture proves anything, it's that He's not afraid of dirt. As a matter of fact, that's where He works!

- In Genesis 2, He breathed in dirt to create life.
- In John 8, He wrote in dirt to protect a sinner.
- In John 9, He spit in dirt to open blind eyes.
- In Luke 8, He used dirt to teach about the condition of our hearts.
- In Luke 23, He fell in the dirt under the weight of a cross on His way to pay for our sins.

Since the beginning, God has done His best work in the dirt, and your situation is no different. If you'll allow Him, He'll come to the dry and disappointing places of your life to pour in His love, mercy, and grace. Then like a potter, His hands will begin to form something new.

Now, that may strike you as odd, because you want Him to put what was broken back together. But you must remember that God isn't a repairman; He's a potter. He doesn't glue our dreams back together; He invites us to be repurposed and formed into something we never expected—all for His glory.

3. Surrender what you still have.

I don't know if you consider yourself "controlling," but I'll openly admit that I'm the president of the controlling club. And that reality has been challenged every time I've been hurt.

In the wake of a trauma, there's a sense of grief over what happened but also over what we no longer control. For me, whether it was when leaders wrongfully rejected my plan to marry Kayla, when elders questioned my legitimacy to lead, or when I was abandoned by someone who claimed they were committed, I grieved the event but also grieved the fact I wasn't in control. This caused me to discover that when control is taken, it brings pain, but when control is surrendered, it brings peace. Not from the fact that I know how everything will work out, but from the fact that my life is in the Potter's hands.

God does the pouring, God does the forming, God does the filling. But He can't do any of it until we surrender. Surrender is nothing more than offering a simple prayer something like Isaiah 64:8: "You, LORD, are our Father. We are the clay, you are the potter; we are all the work of your hand." If you sincerely pray this prayer and surrender your pain, then God is given the green light to go to work transforming your situation.

I realize saying this prayer is easier than walking it out, because you're signing on to receive a destiny you may have never envisioned, in a place you've never been, with people you've yet to meet. But that's where faith comes in. You must trust that God sees something you don't.

Consider the difference in your emotions as you watch the news compared to when you watch the History Channel. When you watch the news, you're concerned, nervous, or even agitated because you don't know how a difficult situation will work out. But when you watch the History Channel, you're relaxed because you know how the story ends. I doubt you've ever heard anyone say, "I'm watching this documentary on the Civil War, and I'm nervous about how the battle at Gettysburg will turn out."

To God, your life is the History Channel. He's not worried or unsure because He isn't trapped in the process; He's outside of it, overseeing it. He doesn't see you from your present mess; He's standing in your future looking at the masterpiece you haver become! And from your future He confidently declares:

- "Your present discomfort is not your destiny" (1 Peter 5:10).
- "You won't live empty; I'll fill up your life, and you'll carry what others need" (John 4:14).
- "Make no mistake about it—you are My masterpiece" (Ephesians 2:10 NLT).

4. Stay put until your new season comes.

God can see the form you take in the days ahead, but for you to see it, you must choose to stay on the potter's wheel. A vase is not a lump of clay that got lucky; it stayed on the wheel long enough and surrendered to the potter's process. While God is remaking you, it can be head-spinning. All you can see is what's undone and how formless and empty you feel. But remember, surrender is never a one-time event. It's done again and again.

God Isn't Finished

In so many moments, I was tempted to give up my place in God's family. The pain people cause sometimes seems unbearable, and the path forward appears too long. But each time—through the tears, trauma, and drama—I settled on the fact that I wanted God's plan for me more than anything else.

I still do. And although I often don't trust His people, God remains trustworthy. Although I've encountered a lot of bad, He remains the definition of good. And although I often grow impatient with the process, He is the potter, and He's not finished.

As we close our time together, my hope is that more than anything else, you'll pursue God's plan for your life and that in your recovery you won't grow impatient. My prayer is that when you doubt the process and struggle to stay, you'll return to this promise: "He who has begun a good work in you will [continue to] perfect and complete it until the day of Christ Jesus [the time of His return]," (Philippians 1:6 AMP).

We may never meet, but I still can't wait to see what God crafts out of your past. I believe your story, like a uniquely designed container filled with cool water, will pour a refreshing grace into those who hear it. But in the meantime, remember this:

Better days are ahead because God's not done!

Acknowledgments

Though my name is on the cover of this book, the truth is it would not exist without the incredible people God has connected me to.

First, Pastor Sam, you've stood on the world's largest platforms, yet you're still servant-hearted enough to open a door. Thank you for opening one for me.

Second, to the team at Baker Publishing Group's Chosen Books, I've never met a more capable, encouraging, and patient group of people. To write is to be vulnerable, and you were a safe place for this dream to find life.

Next, to the Twin Rivers staff and family, you have given me more than I could have ever given you. When you received me all those years ago, I had very little confidence. But you let me borrow yours, and for that I am forever grateful.

Finally, I want to express my immense gratitude to my family. To my sisters, Rachael and Katy, thank you for always saying "Yes!" To my children—Sawyer, Ellee, Sydney, Remi, and Caroline—one of my main motivations was to make you proud. To Kayla, I struggle to find words to convey how much you mean to me (which is ironic considering how many words are in this book). You prayed this project through, therefore, you will share in every heart that's healed!

Notes

Chapter 1 It's Time to Tackle the Problem

1. Bonnie Kristian, "What If Churches Ask for More and No One Says Yes?" *Christianity Today*, August 4, 2023, https://www.christianitytoday.com/ct/2023/august-web-only/jake-meador-atlantic-great-dechurching-us-attendance-stats.html.

2. Kaushik Patowary, "Shrek, The Sheep Who Escaped Shearing for 6 Years," *Amusing Planet*, July 23, 2014, https://www.amusingplanet.com/2014/07/shrek-sheep-who-escaped-shearing-for-6.html.

Chapter 3 The Risk of Remaining Hurt

1. Barna, "Most American Christians Do Not Believe That Satan or the Holy Spirit Exist," April 13, 2009, https://www.barna.com/research/most-american-christians-do-not-believe-that-satan-or-the-holy-spirit-exist.

Chapter 4 Hypocrisy

1. Brennan Manning, *The Ragamuffin Gospel: Good News for the Bedraggled, Beat-Up, and Burnt Out* (Colorado Springs: Multnomah, 2008), 48.

2. Jeanne Mcdowell, "Behavior: True Confessions by Telephone," *Time*, October 03, 1988, https://content.time.com/time/subscriber/article/0,33009,968598,00.html.

Chapter 5 Judgmentalism

1. Josh Packard and Ashleigh Hope, *Church Refugees: Sociologists Reveal Why People Are DONE with Church but Not Their Faith* (Loveland, CO: Group Publishing, 2015), 59.

2. Paddy Dinham, "London Police Stop Man Jumping from North Circular Bridge," *Daily Mail*, April 28, 2017, https://www.dailymail.co.uk/news/article-4456800/Police-stop-man-jumping-North-Circular-bridge.html.

3. Red Johnson, "Ark of the Covenant and the Actual Value of the Gold in King Solomon's Temple!" From The Exodus To The Ridiculous, July 29, 2017, https://exodusmyth.com/2017/07/29/ark-of-the-covenant-and-the-actual-value-of-the-gold-in-king-solomons-temple.

4. Lambert Dolphin, "The Treasures of the House of the Lord," Temple Mount, July 16, 2021, https://www.templemount.org/TMTRS.html.

5. "Help Us Remember," Beliefnet, accessed December 7, 2023, https://www.beliefnet.com/prayers/protestant/compassion/help-us-remember.aspx.

Chapter 6 Rejection

1. Guy Winch, "Why Rejection Hurts So Much—and What to Do about It," TED, December 8, 2015, https://ideas.ted.com/why-rejection-hurts-so-much-and-what-to-do-about-it.

2. C. S. Lewis, *Mere Christianity* (United Kingdom: HarperCollins, 2001), 50. *Mere Christianity* by CS Lewis © copyright 1942, 1943, 1944, 1952 CS Lewis Pte Ltd. Extract used with permission.

Chapter 7 Sexual Abuse: Acknowledging the Pain

1. Mark A. Blais and Sheila M. O'Keefe, "Understanding and Applying Psychological Assessment," Massachusetts General Hospital Comprehensive Clinical Psychiatry, 2008, https://www.sciencedirect.com/topics/medicine-and-dentistry/controlled-oral-word-association-test.

2. Antony J. Blinken, "National Human Trafficking Prevention Month 2023: Press Statement," U.S. Department of State, January 19, 2023, https://www.state.gov/national-human-trafficking-prevention-month-2023.

3. Dan B. Allender, *The Wounded Heart: Hope for Adult Victims of Childhood Sexual Abuse* (Carol Stream, IL: NavPress, 2018), 47.

4. United States Department of Health and Human Services, Administration for Children and Families, Administration on Children, Youth and Families, Children's Bureau. Child Maltreatment Survey, 2016 (2018), https://www.acf.hhs.gov/cb/report/child-maltreatment-2016.

5. H. M. Zinzow, H. S. Resnick, J. L. McCauley, A. B. Amstadter, K. J. Ruggiero, D. G. Kilpatrick, "Prevalence and Risk of Psychiatric Disorders As a Function of Variant Rape Histories: Results from a National Survey of Women," *Social Psychiatry and Psychiatric Epidemiology*, 47(6), 893–902 (2012).

6. Allender, *Wounded Heart*, 111.

Chapter 8 Sexual Abuse: Overcoming Shame

1. Jimmy Evans with Frank Martin, *When Life Hurts: Finding Hope and Healing from the Pain You Carry* (Grand Rapids, MI: Baker Books, 2013), 71.

Chapter 9 Disappointment with Leaders

1. Rasmus Hougaard, "The Real Crisis in Leadership," *Forbes*, September 9, 2018, https://www.forbes.com/sites/rasmushougaard/2018/09/09/the-real-crisis-in-leadership/?sh=24b5bbae3ee4.

2. William Arruda, "What Employees Really Think about Their Bosses," *Forbes*, December 12, 2017, https://www.forbes.com/sites/williamarruda/2017/12/12/what-employees-really-think-about-their-boss/?sh=2b778ce6a1ec.

3. Justin McCarthy, "In U.S, Trust in Politicians, Voters Continues to Ebb," Gallup, October 7, 2021, https://doi.org/https://news.gallup.com/poll/355430/trust-politicians-voters-continues-ebb.aspx.

4. Jeffery M. Jones, "Confidence in U.S. Institutions Down; Average at New Low," Gallup, July 5, 2022, https://doi.org/https://news.gallup.com/poll/394283/confidence-institutions-down-average-new-low.aspx.

5. C. S. Lewis, *Reflections on the Psalms* (New York: Harcourt, Brace, 1958), 32. *Reflections on the Psalms* by CS Lewis © copyright 1958 CS Lewis Pte Ltd. Extract used with permission.

Chapter 10 Wounding Words

1. Prakhar Verma, "Destroy Negativity from Your Mind with This Simple Exercise," Medium, November 27, 2017, https://medium.com/the-mission/a-practical-hack-to-combat-negative-thoughts-in-2-minutes-or-less-cc3d1bddb3af.

Chapter 11 Unresolved Conflict

1. Dr. Gurmon shared this insight with me in a personal email, and I share it here with his permission.

2. Robert Plutchik, "The Nature of Emotions: Human Emotions Have Deep Evolutionary Roots, a Fact That May Explain Their Complexity and Provide Tools for Clinical Practice," *American Scientist* 89, No. 4 (2001): 344–50.

3. Rick Warren, "Seven Biblical Steps to Resolving Conflict," Pastors.com, May 17, 2023, https://pastors.com/seven-biblical-steps-to-resolving-conflict/.

Chapter 12 Loneliness and Isolation

1. Selby Frame, "Julianne Holt-Lunstad Probes Loneliness, Social Connections," American Psychological Association, October 18, 2017, https://www.apa.org/members/content/holt-lunstad-loneliness-social-connections.

2. C. S. Lewis, *Letters to Malcolm: Chiefly on Prayer* (New York: Harcourt, Brace, and World, 1964), 93. *Letters to Malcolm* by CS Lewis © copyright 1963, 1964 CS Lewis Pte Ltd. Extract used with permission.

3. Betty-Ann Heggie, "The Healing Power of Laughter," *Journal of Hospital Medicine*, May 14, 2019, https://www.ncbi.nlm.nih.gov/pmc/articles/PMC6609137.

Chapter 13 Develop Staying Power

1. Graeme Hamilton, "Attendance at Religious Services Lowers Risk of Depression, Study Finds," *National Post*, April 2013, https://nationalpost.com/holy-post/attendance-at-religious-services-lowers-risk-of-depression-study-finds.

2. Tyler J. VanderWeele and John Siniff, "Religion May Be a Miracle Drug: Column," *USA Today*, October 28, 2016, https://www.usatoday.com/story/opinion/2016/10/28/religion-church-attendance-mortality-column/92676964.

3. Mark D. Regnerus and Glen H. Elder Jr., "Staying on Track in School: Religious Influences in High- and Low-Risk Settings," *Journal for the Scientific Study of Religion* 42, no. 4 (2003): 633–49, http://www.jstor.org/stable/1387912.

4. Jamie Ducharme, "You Asked: Do Religious People Live Longer?" *Time*, February 15, 2018, https://time.com/5159848/do-religious-people-live-longer.

5. Elizabeth Flock, "Devout Catholics Have Better Sex, Study Says," *U.S. News*, July 17, 2013, https://www.usnews.com/news/articles/2013/07/17/devout-catholics-have-better-sex.

6. Gallup Editors, "Most Americans Practice Charitable Giving, Volunteerism," Gallup News, December 13, 2013, https://news.gallup.com/poll/166250/americans-practice-charitable-giving-volunteerism.aspx.

Chapter 14 Be Responsible for Your Own Growth

1. Ryan Foley, "Scripture Engaged Christians 'Flourish in Every Domain of Human Experience': Survey," *Christian Post*, June 12, 2023, https://www.christianpost.com/news/faithful-christians-flourish-in-all-aspects-of-life-survey.html.

Chapter 15 Embrace a Flexible Faith

1. Jaron Schneider, "Kodak Says It's Committed to Making Film As Long As There Is Demand," PetaPixel, August 14, 2023, https://petapixel.com/2023/08/14/kodak-says-its-committed-to-making-film-as-long-as-there-is-demand.

Chapter 16 Commit to Unity

1. Viktor Frankl, *Man's Search for Meaning* (Boston: Beacon Press, 2006), 31, 33–36.

2. John C. Maxwell, *The 360 Degree Leader: Developing Your Influence from Anywhere in the Organization* (Nashville: Thomas Nelson, 2006), 78.

3. Miles McPherson, *The Third Option* (New York: Howard Books, 2020), 112–13.

Chapter 17 Reach Out in Love

1. "The Charles Blondin Story," Creative Bible Study, accessed December 7, 2023, https://www.creativebiblestudy.com/Blondin-story.html.

2. Joe Aldridge, *Lifestyle Evangelism: Learning to Open Your Life to Those around You* (Colorado Springs: Multnomah Books, 1981), 19.

Conclusion Mess to Masterpiece

1. Vernon D. Swaback, "Frank Lloyd Wright's Greatest Work," *The Whirling Arrow* (blog), Frank Lloyd Wright Foundation, May 16, 2017, https://franklloyd wright.org/frank-lloyd-wrights-greatest-work.

2. Brian G. Skotko, Susan P. Levine, and Richard Goldstein, "Self-perceptions from People with Down Syndrome," *American Journal of Medical Genetics* Part A, no. 10 (2011): 2360, accessed September 16, 2023, https://doi.org/10.1002/ajmg.a.34235.

3. Phil Hansen, "Embrace the Shake," TED, February 2013, https://www.ted.com/talks/phil_hansen_embrace_the_shake.

Joe Dobbins and his wife, Kayla, serve as the lead pastors of TwinRivers Church in St. Louis, Missouri. Twin Rivers engages thousands of people each week through multiple campuses and is known for its commitment to serving the community through radical generosity.

Pastor Joe has a sincere passion for strengthening churches and leaders. He has served many organizations, denominations, and local churches by expanding their leadership and ministry strategies. He serves on the Church of God International Executive Council, which in turn serves more than eight million people globally. He also holds a seat on the Board of Trustees for Oral Robert University in Tulsa, Oklahoma.

Pastor Joe, Kayla, and their five children love the city of St. Louis and proudly call it home.

For more information, leadership materials,
or to submit a speaking request:

JoeDobbins.org